# The
# CORPORAL
### &
# SPIRITUAL
# Works *of* Mercy

D0967887

# The
# CORPORAL
# *&*
# SPIRITUAL
# Works *of* Mercy

## *Living Christian Love and Compassion*

## MITCH FINLEY

Liguori
LIGUORI, MISSOURI

Published by Liguori Publications
Liguori, Missouri
www.liguori.org
www.catholicbooksonline.com

Copyright © 2003 by Mitch Finley

All rights reserved. No part of this publication may be reproduced, stored in a retrieval system, or transmitted in any form or by any means—electronic, mechanical, photocopy, recording, or any other—except for brief quotations in printed reviews, without the prior permission of the publishers.

**Library of Congress Cataloging-in-Publication Data**

Finley, Mitch.
    The corporal and spiritual works of mercy : living Christian love and compassion / Mitch Finley.—1st ed.
        p. cm.
    Includes bibliographical references.
    ISBN 0-7648-0840-0 (pbk.)
    1. Corporal works of mercy. 2. Spiritual works of mercy. 3. Catholic Church—Doctrines. I. Title.

BV4647.M4F56 2003
241—dc21                                    2003044620

Scripture quotations are taken from the *New Revised Standard Version Bible*, copyright 1989 by the Division of Christian Education of the National Council of the Churches of Christ in the U.S.A. Used by permission. All rights reserved.

By Thomas Merton, from *The Collected Poems of Thomas Merton*, copyright © 1963 by The Abbey of Gethsemani, Inc. Reprinted by permission of New Directions Publishing Corp. Sales Territory: U.S., Canadian and open market rights only. For British Commonwealth rights (excluding Canada), refer to: Gerald Pollinger, Ltd. 9 Staple Inn, Holborn, London WC1V 7QH, United Kingdom.

English translation of the *Catechism of the Catholic Church* for the United States of America, copyright © 1994, United States Catholic Conference, Inc.—Libreria Editrice Vaticana. English translation of the *Catechism of the Catholic Church: Modifications from the Editio Typica*, copyright © 1997, United States Catholic Conference, Inc.—Libreria Editrice Vaticana. Used with permission.

Printed in the United States of America
08 07 06 05 04 03   5 4 3 2 1
First edition

# Contents

# Introduction

Time was, Catholic schools and parish CCD programs[1] required kids to memorize and recite the "corporal works of mercy" and the "spiritual works of mercy." A glance at the Contents page of this book will tell you the items that appeared on each list. The idea, as with so much of the catechetical theory that predominated in the pre-Vatican II Catholic Church, was that to memorize it was to know it, and to know it was to believe it, and to believe it was to practice it. While this approach to catechetics may have had more going for it than the post-Vatican II enthusiasm for experiential catechetics gave it credit for, still, catechists probably expected too much of it all by itself.

There was nothing wrong with these two lists of ways to be merciful. Indeed, this book presupposes that the two lists still have considerable value. The presupposition has always been that to live out the "works of mercy" was the whole point. All the same, there is a basic assumption behind the two lists of "corporal" and "spiritual" works of mercy that we do well to examine with a critical eye. Indeed, this assumption led to the development of two separate lists rather than one single list.

The underlying assumption was that there were two ways to be merciful. The first way to be merciful was "corporal," a word based on the Latin *corpus*, body. Thus, "corporal" works of mercy refer to "bodily" or "physical" ways of being merciful.

The second way to be merciful was spiritual. Thus, "spiritual" works of mercy refer to being merciful in ways that have an impact on the soul. In other words, the two lists presuppose that people are made up of two parts, a body and a soul. Thus, "works of mercy" could be aimed at either a person's body or soul. In other words, the traditional lists of the corporal and spiritual works of mercy are *dualistic*, they take for granted that the human person has two separate parts that are only incidentally related, a body and a soul.

Anyone who has not been living under a literal or metaphorical cabbage leaf since the late 1960s knows, however, that this dualistic view of the human person no longer resonates with actual human experience, if it ever did—not to mention the works of philosophers and theologians; not to mention the official understanding of the Catholic Church. Today, we take for granted the unity of body and soul; today, to recall the words of theologian Karl Rahner, S.J., we presume that the human person is an embodied spirit. To quote the *Catechism of the Catholic Church*:

> The human person, created in the image of God, is a being at once corporeal and spiritual....
> 
> The unity of the soul and body is so profound that one has to consider the soul to be the "form" of the body: i.e., it is because of its spiritual soul that the body made of matter becomes a living, human body; spirit and matter, in man, are not two natures united, but rather their union forms one single nature.[2]

It's all a profound mystery, of course, this business of being "embodied spirits." Even this understanding fails to do complete justice to our experience of being human. Still, it serves better than the older, dualistic concept. To act in merciful ways toward others, whether the specific way of being merciful falls under the category of "corporal" or "spiritual," has an effect on the whole person, body and soul. To feed those who are hungry has not only a bodily impact but a spiritual one, too. To comfort someone who is sorrowful gives not only spiritual comfort but a comfort that he or she can feel physically, too.

As we move into our reflections on the corporal and spiritual works of mercy, we do well to keep uppermost in our consciousness this body-soul unity. As we ponder each of the works of mercy we shall see that to practice each one is to communicate the mercy of Christ in ways that have both bodily and spiritual effects. What, then, is the value of maintaining two separate lists? Why not just call them all "works of mercy" and let it go at that? Indeed, the *Catechism of the Catholic Church* does precisely this. "The *works of mercy* are charitable actions by which we come to the aid of our neighbor in his spiritual and bodily necessities."[3] Because many Catholics still recognize the old distinction, however, and as a way to organize the material in this book, we will retain the two lists of corporal and spiritual works of mercy.

Finally, it is important to notice that the corporal and spiritual works of mercy are deeply rooted in Scripture and sacred Tradition. As we get into our discussion of each of the works of mercy, these connections will become clear. To turn our attention to these two traditional lists of ways to be merciful is to zero in on the heart and soul of a practical Christian spirituality and way of life. This is a spirituality for regular folks who live in the real, everyday world. It's a spirituality and a practical program of faith for the home and the workplace and all the ordinary places in-between that we all inhabit on a daily basis. It's a nitty-gritty spirituality, and there is nothing ethereal about it. So, spiritually speaking, pull on your bib overalls, strap on your boots, and don your construction site helmet, because we're about to explore Catholic spirituality as it takes shape in its most knockabout ways.

# The
# CORPORAL
# Works *of* Mercy

CHAPTER I

# To Feed the Hungry

The corporal works of mercy are particularly easy to trace to the Scriptures. Indeed, most of them come directly from the familiar words of Jesus in the parable of the sheep and the goats in the Gospel of Matthew, and among them "to feed the hungry" takes first place:

> "Then the king will say to those at his right hand, 'Come, you that are blessed by my Father, inherit the kingdom prepared for you from the foundation of the world; for I was hungry and you gave me food...'" (Mt 25:34–35).

Nothing is more basic and necessary to human existence than physical nourishment. Yet it's no secret that countless people in our world go to sleep and wake up hungry day after day. So prominent is this issue in today's world that the *Catechism of the Catholic Church* addresses it twice in explicit terms. First, the catechism relates hunger in the world directly to a violation of the fifth commandment ("You shall not kill"):

> The acceptance by human society of murderous famines, without efforts to remedy them, is a scandalous

injustice and a grave offense. Those whose usurious
and avaricious dealings lead to the hunger and death
of their brethren in the human family indirectly commit homicide, which is imputable to them.[4]

Strong words, indeed. Those who live in the wealthier, so-
called "developed" nations do well to take to heart the *Catechism*'s
use of the terms "usury" and "avarice." It takes only a little
investigation to discover that the United States, for example,
consumes far more than its share of the world's resources, to
the point that it becomes impossible to avoid using unpleasant
sounding words like "usurious" and "avaricious." It becomes
impossible to not ask why such a wealthy nation will not forgive poor nations the debts they owe this wealthy nation, huge
debts the payments on which help to keep poor nations stuck
in their poverty.

Second, the *Catechism* makes a direct connection between
world hunger and the petition in the Our Father to "give us
this day our daily bread." Thus

...the drama of hunger in the world calls Christians
who pray sincerely to exercise responsibility toward
their brethren, both in their personal behavior and in
their solidarity with the human family.[5]

These words relate personal behavior to world hunger. In
other words, there is a connection between personal choices
we make about consumption and the fact that countless people
never get enough food to eat. To practice the corporal work of
mercy called "feeding the hungry" requires that we not only
give to our local food bank and send donations to agencies
that try to feed the hungry in distant lands, it also requires that
we ask what we can do to change our personal habits of consumption. This is one of the most basic applications of the

wise advice to "think globally and act locally." It's natural to feel helpless when it comes to "world hunger." It's easier to believe that we can have an impact if we think in terms of what we can do in our little corner of the world.

True story: When Mari was a girl of twelve she attended a Catholic school in a small community in Idaho. One day Mari's teacher asked the class to think of ways they could help with the problem of world hunger. The class had watched videos, done some research on the Internet, and read a magazine article, and they were at a point in their experience as a class where they were feeling overwhelmed by the enormity of the problem. What on earth could a few kids in a little school in rural Idaho do to get more food to people who were starving on the other side of the world?

Mari's teacher suggested that the class brainstorm responses. Students suggested obvious ideas, such as sending donations of money to agencies that send food to people who don't get enough to eat. Then Mari had a bright idea. "Why couldn't we send food to someplace where it's needed ourselves, without going through some big organization?" she asked. "My dad works at the grain elevator. Maybe he could get farmers to donate wheat or something like that...."

Mari's teacher suggested that Mari talk with her father that evening and report to the class the next day. When Mari explained to her father about the discussion her class had and the problem of hunger, he listened sympathetically. "But Mari," he said, "I don't know if the farmers would want to do this, and it would be a big job to get the wheat to the people who need it."

There would be a meeting of the farmer's cooperative the following week, however, and Mari's father agreed to let her and a few of her classmates speak at the meeting. When the time for the meeting finally arrived, Mari and three of her classmates stood before a room full of adults and explained that they wanted to help feed hungry people in a distant country. Would the farmers be willing to help by donating some of their crops, and would the cooperative be willing to help by finding a way to ship the grain to the people who needed it?

After some discussion, Mari's father announced to the gathering that he thought it would be possible to do what his daughter and her classmates had suggested. He would make some phone calls the following day. In the end, an entire shipload of wheat found its way to hungry people on the other side of the world, and all because a little girl in Idaho imagined that it might be possible.

Of course, even what Mari was able to spark can, in the long run, be called only a temporary help. Ultimately, the problem of world hunger is much more complicated. It is a problem not of the world being able to produce enough food to feed all the people in the world. Economists and other experts agree that this is not the case. Rather, it's a problem of the fair distribution of the world's food so that everyone gets enough to eat.

All the same, in the meantime people are hungry, and not just in distant lands. Even in the affluent western nations hunger exists, and numerous agencies try to alleviate hunger in all the ways they can. Most towns and cities have a food bank of some sort where people who are hungry and without other alternatives can go to get at least a little relief. Often, too, churches and charitable organizations sponsor soup kitchens and hot meal programs. For many years, for example, St. Benedict the Moor Parish, in Milwaukee, Wisconsin, has been the home of a hot meal program six evenings a week. Men, women, and children line up evening after evening to get a hot meal.

One of the most admirable things about the hot meal program at St. Ben's is the fact that it gets its support, in large part, from the participation of people from throughout the entire Milwaukee area. Ordinary middle-class men, women, and children prepare and serve the meal each evening that St. Ben's is open. Thus, ordinary people carry out this most basic of the corporal works of mercy, and it's not just a matter of the affluent serving the poor. Everyone sits down together to share the meal, and it's not unusual for those who have been served—the street people, the homeless, the poor—once they have eaten to take a place in the serving line so that someone else can sit down and eat. At St. Ben's, everyone serves and everyone is served. Children learn non-classroom lessons here.

Sometimes there can be a tendency, however, to distance the corporal works of mercy from the real world, or to turn them into a list of "heroic virtues" that seem to have little to do with a faith that lives in the everyday world. There can be a tendency to think of the corporal works of mercy as character-istic of the lives of the greatest saints but not having much to do with the lives of ordinary believers. On the contrary, more often than not, those who "feed the hungry" are to be found in the most ordinary places, and they rarely think of them-selves as practicing a corporal work of mercy.

Parents who work to earn the money to buy the groceries for the family are feeding the hungry as surely as anyone who volunteers at an inner city soup kitchen or a food bank. Fa-thers and mothers who prepare meal after meal, who pack school lunch after school lunch, day after day for years and years, practice the work of mercy called "feeding the hungry." Most of the time, however, they don't give it a second thought, and they certainly don't think of themselves as doing anything particularly virtuous. Still, what they do is feed the hungry, and they would do well, now and then, to give themselves a little credit for what they do. Priests and deacons who hold forth homiletically at Sunday Masses would do well, now and then, to give such folks a verbal pat on the back.

Yet another way we can knock the patina of a superficial

piety off the notion of feeding the hungry is to look for other ways we can give credit where credit is due. When we think of those whose daily work is dedicated to caring for and serving others, we tend first to think of doctors, nurses, and other medical service professions. We may think of teachers and counselors, too. But how often do we think of those who grow the food we need in order to survive?

When we think of those who give their lives to serving others, how often do we think, in particular, of those who struggle in our own time to keep family farms going? The family farm is at risk, big-time, these days, and yet so much of the food we find in supermarkets comes from family farms. Truly, the family farm is a family project dedicated to feeding the hungry, and we need to give more credit to the families who dedicate their lives to the family farm as a going concern.

How often, when we think of feeding the hungry, do we think of those who take it as their concern to call into question the quality of the foods we eat? What about people who call our attention to the chemicals that are often used to spray or fertilize the crops, who ask what the long-range impact will be on the health of all of us who eat these foods? Concern for the quality of the food people consume is yet another way to feed the hungry in today's world.

People sometimes find with creative ways to help feed the hungry. Take, for example, a national program called Plant a Row for the Hungry (PAR). This is a public service campaign of the Garden Writers Association of America that is sponsored by local organizations. The idea is to get backyard gardeners to plant an extra row of vegetables, herbs, or fruit to donate to local food banks. In the summer of 2000, the program's first year in Spokane, Washington, local gardeners donated about seven thousand pounds of fresh produce.[6]

Guidelines for Plant a Row for the Hungry instruct gardeners to choose produce that can sit on food bank shelves for twenty-four to forty-eight hours and still be usable. This is because food banks often don't have enough refrigerated space to store all the produce that comes in. Tomatoes, broccoli, corn, potatoes, and carrots are ideal choices.

There are many ways to "feed the hungry," however, and the last thing we should do is limit our understanding of this way of being merciful to literal, face-value interpretations. Even the old *Baltimore Catechism* draws our attention to a wider and deeper perspective:

> One can feed the hungry…not only by actually providing the necessities of life by also by working to correct economic abuses which cause unnecessary unemployment and poverty.[7]

The Catholic Church's teachings on social and economic justice are anything but incidental to the corporal works of mercy, including the need to feed the hungry. Clearly, there is always a need to bring immediate relief to those who are hungry here and now. There is a need for soup kitchens, food banks, and hot meal programs. But there is also a need to work to bring about social and economic change that will result in the elimination of the *causes* of hunger. There is a need for politicians willing to work for these social and economic changes. There is a need for political activists who try to "shake up the system" in order to bring about social and economic change. Politicians and social activists who work for such changes "feed the hungry" just as surely as those who staff the soup kitchens, hot meal programs, and food banks.

Any lingering doubt about the centrality of feeding the hungry to a Christian life gives way to the fact that one of the rare accounts of an event in the life of Jesus that appears in all four gospels is the story about Jesus feeding a large crowd with but a few loaves of bread and a few fish. The accounts differ slightly in each gospel, but the essentials are there in all four. In the Gospel of John (6:5), Jesus himself raises the question of where they are going to get food for the crowd to eat. In the synoptic Gospels, the disciples ask Jesus to send the people off to find nourishment for themselves. In the oldest gospel, Mark, for example: "When it grew late, his disciples came to him and said, 'This is a deserted place, and the hour is now very late; send them away so that they may go into the surrounding country and villages and buy something for themselves to eat'" (6:35–36).

Jesus, however, has "compassion" (6:34) on the crowd and refuses to send the people away. Instead, he directs the disciples to find food for the crowd: "You give them something to eat" (6:37). Then, when the disciples plead helplessness, the gospel tells us that Jesus feeds the "great crowd" (6:34) with five loaves of bread and two fish (6:38). Mark then comments: "And all ate and were filled; and they took up twelve baskets full of broken pieces and of the fish. Those who had eaten the loaves numbered five thousand men" (6:42–44).

Apart from the clear eucharistic overtones of the account of the feeding of the crowd with a few loaves and fish, there is no doubt that Jesus had concern for the basic human need for food, and he did not view this need as one that his disciples could dismiss as the responsibility of the people themselves. Jesus did not say, "Hey, if they're hungry they should have thought about that before they left home; they should have brought sack lunches. It's not my responsibility to feed these people if they are so forgetful. If I feed them I'm just going to be encouraging irresponsibility. Talk about encouraging co-dependence! No way!"

Jesus does not ask if the people deserve to eat. The people are hungry, and that's all that matters. It is the responsibility of his disciples to feed the hungry, no questions asked. The lesson is one that Christians down through the centuries have taken to heart. If people are hungry, you do what you can to feed them. You don't ask if they deserve it or not. You don't accuse hungry people of being lazy or irresponsible for getting themselves into a situation where they need to rely on others for food. You just feed them.

In a letter that predates by some twenty years even Mark, the earliest gospel, Saint Paul declares to his readers that those who are disciples of Christ should feed even those who are against them: "...if your enemies are hungry, feed them; if they are thirsty, give them something to drink..." (Rom 12:20). This is the crunch point that distinguishes the Christian from the charitable humanist. To be a disciple of Christ is to make no distinction between hungry friend and hungry enemy. To relieve hunger is the only concern.

The fourth-century Egyptian monk and saint, Serapion, once sold his copy of the Gospels and gave the money to those who were hungry. He said: "I have sold the book that told me to sell all that I had and give to the poor."[8]

Thus, the issue of hunger, and the fact that the first corporal work of mercy is to feed the hungry, actually brings us face to face with one of the most basic principles of the Christian life. It goes something like this: The most basic characteristic of a Christian is not that he or she attends Mass every Sunday. Rather, the most basic characteristic of a Christian is that the foundation of his or her life is the love of God and neighbor. Only then does attending Mass take its proper place in the life of faith and, indeed, becomes indispensable. The one who attends Mass consistently, every Sunday—or even every day— but does not strive at all times to love God and neighbor is no disciple of Christ.

To feed the hungry is the simplest, most basic, and most essential corporal work of mercy. A Christian faith that is authentic requires this act of mercy in one form or another, always and everywhere.

## CHAPTER 2

# To Give Drink to the Thirsty

Once again we find ourselves smack in the heart of the story of the sheep and the goats in Matthew 25. The second corporal work of mercy, to give drink to the thirsty, almost seems redundant. If we're going to feed the hungry it only stands to reason that we should give them something to drink, as well. If we make this assumption, however, we may be overlooking some important insights. More often than not, if Scripture seems to do something unnecessary or redundant the contrary proves to be true. If we are told that we should not only feed the hungry but give drink to the thirsty, most likely there is a reason for this apparent redundancy.

The human experience of thirst is, after all, not identical with the experience of hunger. It's perfectly possible to be thirsty but not hungry, or vice versa. We may be rewarded with some unique insights, then, if we don't just skim over this second work of mercy but try to take a close look at it. For starters, reflect for a moment on the experience of being thirsty and the circumstances that can lead to thirst.

If you feel thirsty it means that you are in need of fluids. For one reason or another, your tongue begins to get that unpleasant, subtle tingling sensation that you immediately identify as the signal that you need something to drink. If you don't get something to quench your thirst this sensation grows stronger. If you go for a long time without water your tongue begins to feel dry. In extreme conditions of deprivation your tongue even begins to swell. Once you get a drink of water, of course, you begin to return to normal.

Thirst comes when you begin to need fluids. This makes perfectly good sense, of course, because without water the human body is in bad shape, indeed. Physically, you are mostly water. Water makes up 50 to 70 percent of the weight of the human body. Even teeth have a water content of 5 percent. Water is the essential medium of all body fluids including digestive juices, lymph, blood, urine, and perspiration. Not only that, but water is necessary to carry essential nutrients for the healthy working of the body. It is also responsible for such functions as temperature regulation within the body and the lubrication of joints.

When the second corporal work of mercy directs us to "give drink to the thirsty" it isn't just being redundant. There is a human need for water that is completely independent of the need for food. When we give drink to the thirsty we provide the stuff of life itself. But, you may ask, whereas sometimes food is difficult to get, water is not. While this is largely true in the places where most of the readers of this book live, there are plenty of places in the world where it's not true at all.

All you need do is visit just about anyplace in Central America or the Caribbean, and you'll see how relatively scarce water fit to drink can be. Those who take for granted hot and cold running water piped into their homes find it difficult to identify with people who must walk a short or long distance to a source of potable water, then carry a filled container back to where they live. One of the projects people in such places find most helpful is any project that helps to make good, clean water more easily accessible.

In other words, it's not difficult for giving drink to the thirsty to become a much bigger deal than just handing a glass of water to someone who happens to want one. Indeed, giving drink to the thirsty could easily become a major international concern. At the same time, however, the issue of maintaining sources of drinkable water has been a major issue in North America, as well.

In the early 1960s, it became obvious that water pollution was visible to everyone in the United States. In 1969, the Cuyahoga River in Ohio actually caught fire spontaneously. Historic Boston Harbor was a virtual cesspool, and so was the Potomac River in Washington, D.C., as well as other rivers, lakes, and coastal areas across the United States. Authorities announced that Lake Erie was dead, and a 1969 oil spill off beautiful Santa Barbara, California, caused major public outrage. All of these events created an upsurge in public support for immediate reforms to end water pollution. Everyone who became involved in this issue was, in effect, carrying out the second corporal work of mercy, giving drink to the thirsty.

In 1972, the U.S. Congress passed the Federal Water Pollution Control Act, usually referred to as the Clean Water Act (CWA). The Clean Water Act launched a national cause: to "restore and maintain the chemical, physical, and biological integrity of the nation's waters."[9] The goals of the new law included the elimination of discharge of pollutants into fishable and swimmable waters by 1983 and also included navigable waters by 1985. Again, everyone involved carried out the second corporal work of mercy.

The Clean Water Act required virtually every city in the U.S. to build and operate a wastewater treatment plant to stop the discharge of raw sewage into waters. The new Environmental Protection Agency (EPA) administered federal funding and offered technical assistance wherever it was needed. States adopted water quality standards with federal supervision to make sure that communities everywhere could have clean water. The law set up a permit granting system to limit industrial and municipal discharges into waterways, and to protect wetlands from destruction.

The bishops of the United States, in their 1991 statement *Renewing the Earth,* refer to, among other environmental concerns, chemicals that pollute rivers and lakes. The bishops remind us that sometimes modern industries contribute to acid rain falling over parklands many hundreds of miles distant, and they caution us with regard to wetlands that disappear before the shovels and bulldozers of developers.

In their document the bishops ponder words from the Book of Genesis: "God saw everything that he had made, and indeed, it was very good" (1:31). Then they call us to a kind of faithfulness that we sometimes overlook: "Men and women... bear a unique responsibility under God: to safeguard the created world and by their creative labor even to enhance it."

Referring often to Pope John Paul II's 1990 World Day of Peace message on "the ecological crisis," the bishops refer to Catholic social teaching and call on everyone to develop a responsible outlook on environmental issues, all of which relate to the human need for good, clean, drinkable water. Among the themes the bishops articulate are a God-centered and sacramental view of all of creation, from the smallest blade of grass to the vast and starry universe; a constant respect for human life; an understanding of the fair and just use of the earth's resources; preferential treatment of the poor; and an understanding of "development" that respects the needs of human beings and the rational limits of technological growth and development.

Throughout the world, Catholic and other Christian charitable groups, local dioceses, and individual parishes put these ideas into actual practice by giving drink to the thirsty in a far from limited sense. These groups help to provide clean drinking water in poor countries, and they focus on their own local rivers, lakes, and wetlands out of respect for the place of water in the grand scheme of things. In some places, they actively support underprivileged neighborhoods that undertake legal action to stop developers from destroying wetlands and polluting sources of clean drinking water.

This gives you an idea of the extent to which giving drink to the thirsty has become a major social, economic, and environmental issue. Perhaps by now it should be obvious that to give drinkable water to anyone is to give the gift of life itself, for life cannot be sustained without water. In a very real sense, therefore, whenever we do anything to support and encourage life we "give drink to the thirsty."

The most familiar New Testament story concerning water is the narrative in the Gospel of John about the encounter of Jesus and the Samaritan woman at Jacob's well. In this story, of course, Jesus talks about water on two levels, the literal and the figurative. The Samaritan woman's interest is in literal water, but Jesus takes the opportunity to talk about "living water," that is, the gift of eternal life:

> So [Jesus] came to a Samaritan city called Sychar, near the plot of ground that Jacob had given to his son Joseph. Jacob's well was there, and Jesus, tired out by his journey, was sitting by the well. It was about noon. A Samaritan woman came to draw water, and Jesus said to her, "Give me a drink." (His disciples had gone to the city to buy food.) The Samaritan woman said to him, "How is it that you, a Jew, ask a drink of me, a woman of Samaria?" (Jews do not share things in common with Samaritans.) Jesus answered her, "If you knew the gift of God, and who it is that is saying to you,

'Give me a drink,' you would have asked him, and he would have given you living water." The woman said to him, "Sir, you have no bucket, and the well is deep. Where do you get that living water? Are you greater than our ancestor Jacob, who gave us the well, and with his sons and his flocks drank from it?" Jesus said to her, "Everyone who drinks of this water will be thirsty again, but those who drink of the water that I will give them will never be thirsty. The water that I will give will become in them a spring of water gushing up to eternal life" (Jn 4:5–14).

There is a scriptural precedent, therefore, if we would see two meanings in the corporal work of mercy that urges us to give drink to the thirsty. Without question, the first meaning relates to the human need for water. That is why this work of mercy is "corporal," or bodily. But if we keep in mind the unity of the human person—that we are, to use theologian Karl Rahner's phrase, "embodied spirits"—then we may also apply this work of mercy on the level that Jesus understands it in the fourth gospel's story of his encounter with the Samaritan woman at Jacob's well. Indeed, given Jesus' use of water as a metaphor for eternal life, and given the sacred use of water in the sacrament of baptism, Christian efforts to give drink to the thirsty may nevermore be separated from Christian efforts to share the gifts of faith and salvation in Christ. As Jesus says in another place in the Gospel of John:

"Very truly, I tell you, no one can enter the kingdom of God without being born of water and Spirit" (3:5).

Is it any wonder, therefore, that water plays such a constant part in Catholic liturgical and devotional life? At the entrances to every church, chapel, cathedral, and basilica there are fonts of one shape or another filled with water that has been blessed—commonly called "holy water." Into this holy water we dip our fingertips and then make the sign of the cross. We do this most often without thinking much about it. It's a simple devotional gesture. But if we stop to reflect on what we do, several levels of meaning become evident.

When we make the sign of the cross with holy water we remind ourselves of our baptism which, of course, requires either that water be poured over our forehead or—more frequently today than in years gone by—our whole body be submerged in water. In the sacrament of baptism water symbolizes and actually gives the grace of new life in Christ. The person being baptized receives the gift of eternal life for which he or she "thirsts" at the very root of his or her being. Thus, the Church gives us the ultimate "drink" for which we thirst, namely, redemption from sin, darkness, and despair.

Indeed, the very heart of the Church's life is the ongoing capacity to give this "drink" to all who "thirst" for it. The risen Christ lives in the midst of the faith community that is the Church. Therefore, this community is the place where, to borrow from the narrative of the Samaritan woman at Jacob's well in the fourth gospel, those who are open to it find "a spring of water gushing up to eternal life" (Jn 4:14). Thus, the faith community "gives drink to the thirsty" in the ultimate and most important sense.

At the same time, because those who make up the Church receive this gift of "water gushing up to eternal life" through their membership in and participation in the life of the Church, they are charged with the mission of carrying this gift into their everyday lives. This is not a gift to keep to oneself but a gift to take into the world—not only into our homes and families, although it belongs there, too—but into the workplace and into the wider community. Through our participation in the life of the world at large, the gift we receive can become the gift we give that makes a difference in how things go in our society and culture.

Nourished by the sacraments and by participation in the life of the faith community in all kinds of ways—socially, educationally, and in terms of service activities, for example—we bring to the wider world the gift of "water gushing up to eternal life." Although we may rarely speak explicitly about our experience of this gift—for we live in a culture where mere verbalizing about faith and religion can be easily dismissed—through our *actions,* our intimacy with the living Christ can have a significant impact on the wide world out there.

Often, of course, the "living water" we share with the world amounts to simple acts of kindness and random gifts of unselfish service. We should not overlook, however, ways to share the "water" of eternal life that the world may perceive as a mere rocking of the boat. Sometimes those who share "water gushing up to eternal life" do so by making a racket when a racket is what's needed. Consider, for example, those who participate in actions meant to draw attention to social injustices of various kinds. Consider those who volunteer their time to help those who are less fortunate. Consider those who write letters to their government representatives to oppose legislation they view as harmful or support legislation they view as helpful.

It's also good to keep in mind the "thirst" that calls for the "water gushing up to eternal life" sometimes takes forms we may not recognize right away. In Isaiah, God identifies himself by his readiness to meet the most basic needs of those who are deprived:

> When the poor and needy seek water, / and there is none, and their tongue is parched with thirst, / I the LORD will answer them, / I the God of Israel will not forsake them. / I will open rivers on the bare heights, / and

fountains in the midst of the valleys; / I will make the wilderness a pool of water, / and the dry land springs of water (41:17–18).

The God of Israel reveals himself as the one who will give drink to the thirsty precisely *when there is nothing to drink*. Not only will God give his people water, but his generosity, compassion, and magnanimity are so great that he will bring rivers into existence where there were none before. He will put fountains where there were none before. This God of mercy will, in the midst of the barren wilderness make a pool of cool water for his people. In places of dryness and aridity, he will make cool springs bubbling with water.

The point here, of course, is to be understood both literally and figuratively. Yes, the God of Israel will give his people water overflowing when they are thirsty. The classic example of this, of course, is the Exodus narrative where God instructs Moses:

> "I will be standing there in front of you on the rock at Horeb. Strike the rock, and water will come out of it, so that the people may drink." Moses did so, in the sight of the elders of Israel (17:6).

Ultimately, however, what God will give his people is *himself*, the gift of divine companionship, protection, and love. When they are most alone, most helpless, most in need, and the future looks the most bleak, then God will give his people the cool waters of a final and ultimate rescue, final and ultimate safety, final and ultimate justice and peace. This is because what they—and we—thirst for above and beyond all things is loving intimacy with the God who, according to the Gospel of John, *is* love. Indeed our physical thirst for water is, or should be, a constant reminder of our ultimate thirst for God.

Just so, when we reflect on the meaning of the corporal work of mercy identified as giving drink to the thirsty we do well to think in the same ultimate terms as the God of Isaiah. At the same time, the symbolic or metaphorical meaning of water depends upon and always comes back to our bodily need for water—good, fresh, clean water. Thus, today those who work to preserve our sources of drinkable water act on this corporal work of mercy most completely.

Finally, if there is one thing religious imperatives, even the corporal works of mercy, can use more of sometimes it's a sense of humor. Take the debatable issue of whether city drinking water supplies should be fluoridated or not. More than a few clean-water activists would, no doubt, line up in the anti-fluoridation camp, and not without cause, perhaps. Still, it's difficult to resist quoting the late comic Pat Paulsen who, in the late 1960s, declared the following in one of his hilarious television "editorials" for the fabled Smothers Brothers Comedy Hour:

> The process of fluoridation—the adding of chemicals to our natural waters such as rivers, lakes, streams, ponds, springs, puddles and even damp spots—is one of the most controversial subjects of our time. It is maintained that fluoridation will aid dental health and prevent cavities. On the other hand, it is a basic fringe that is emory and tham and makes a drige close.
>
> Let's get to the faction that does not want to fluoridate our rivers. They claim fluoride chemicals are poisonous. To these people, I say "I hope so." Maybe the poison in the water will kill all the garbage. These are the same people who maintain that fluoride chemicals do not help maintain good teeth. They say our lakes and streams have never been fluoridated—and who's ever seen a guppy with cavities?...Digest that for a

moment....Let's continue to look at the bad side of fluoridation. In Cleveland, Ohio, fluoride was put into the drinking water in 1822—and not one of those people is alive today.

And, of course, we can refer to the test case which is now before the Supreme Court. *Allan B. Farnsworth, D.D.S.* v *Toothless Tommy Tinker*. Much testimony has come to wages the worst size of the master in your mouth....The case is strong for fluoridation. For those of you who don't drink water, I suggest you fluoridate your booze. It won't prevent cavities, but you'll have a mouthful of happy teeth.[10]

There is plenty of room to take seriously the need to "give drink to the thirsty." There are more than enough opportunities to understand this corporal work of mercy both literally and theologically. At the same time, however, along with anything and everything that can be called "religion" humor like that of Pat Paulsen's reminds us that we don't worship or give ultimate concern to religion.[11] Rather, only God deserves our worship and our ultimate concern, so there are times when we can and should laugh about our flailing attempts to live out the corporal work of mercy; for in given instances, no matter how sincerely we think we are right, it's still possible that we could be wrong.

CHAPTER 3

# To Clothe the Naked

A few times each year, the mother of the family would go through her children's clothes and collect together all the items that were too small for any of the other children to wear, as well as any that simply were not being worn for whatever reason. She would then put all the clothing she had collected into paper bags and call the local office of the Saint Vincent de Paul Society and ask for a pickup.

One day, as the family's precocious five-year-old son observed all this, he asked his mother what she was doing. "I'm getting together all the clothes you kids don't wear to give to Saint Vinney's, so poor children who need clothes can have them to wear."

"But," said the little boy, "poor children don't need old clothes; they already have old clothes. They need *new* clothes." To which the mother of the family could only agree.

"I guess you're right," she said. "But your father and I can't afford to clothe other people's kids in addition to our own. As it is, we sometimes have to make you kids wait a few weeks when you need a new pair of shoes, for example."

If this woman were to hear a homily in church that touched on this corporal work of mercy, most likely she would squirm a bit, thinking that there should be more she and her husband could do to "clothe the naked." She would probably think to herself that they don't do a very good job of carrying out this particular work of mercy. In this, however, she would be mistaken.

Parents often need to be reminded that simply by being good parents they find themselves in a position almost daily to act out the corporal works of mercy—and the spiritual ones, too, as we'll see when we get to them. If parents don't "clothe the naked," then no one does! Parents need to give themselves more credit for living out their faith and acting on the heart of the gospel, day in and day out, than they ordinarily do. The fact that they keep growing children in clothes and shoes, not to mention winter coats, is as close to a perfect observance of this corporal work of mercy as anyone is likely to get. It's only an added credit, as it were, when such parents try to pass along to whoever they can the clothing their own children can no longer use.

At the same time, in the dominant western popular culture sometimes this business of clothing the naked takes on dimensions that become strange in the extreme. Parents find themselves under considerable pressure not to just keep their kids in clothing but to keep them in line with dictates of the mass market fashion industry. From the time kids are as young as six or seven, already the pressure to conform to these dictates is considerable. By the time kids are ten or twelve years old, it becomes a major issue. For parents, "to clothe the naked" becomes "to keep the clothed fashionable." Clearly, however, the shift from clothing the naked to keeping the clothed fashionable is not one that can rely on the gospel to justify itself.

Here is where Christian parents can help their adolescents learn to recognize the difference between the gospel and the popular culture; can help them to see that sometimes living our Christian faith can bring us into conflict with values that come from elsewhere. Of course, there is no need to insist that teens must dress as if they were Amish—although the example of the Amish refusal to attend to the dictates of the fashion industry is a worthy one to point out. But parents can gently guide teens, by word *and example*, into recognizing the futility and spiritual emptiness that come with taking "fashion" too seriously.

With good reason, however, this corporal work of mercy receives considerable attention from church social service agencies everywhere. In Philadelphia, Pennsylvania, for example, as in virtually all dioceses, there are ongoing efforts to get warm clothing to those who need it the most during the cold winter months. Philadelphia's Mercy Works Service Projects are scheduled at different times throughout the year, for one day each, to remind everyone of the need to practice the works of mercy all the time.

For example, the Mercy Works Service Project—Clothe the Naked is a one-day event that offers all who are able an opportunity to donate clothing to those who are less fortunate. This Mercy Works Service Project takes place each autumn for one day, with drop-off locations in various parishes. In this Mercy Works Service Project the archdiocese collaborates with the Saint Vincent de Paul Society, which collects clothes throughout the year to benefit those in need.

Many ordinary people donate usable clothing, but special opportunities exist for those who want to continue living out the corporal work of mercy which directs us to clothe the naked. The program recruits volunteers to fold the donated clothes on the day of the collection. This one-day Mercy Works Service Project is based upon already existing, year-round archdiocesan volunteer efforts and is intended to be a reminder that we are called upon to serve our neighbor all year long.

In other words, in our particular historical and cultural situation dioceses like the Archdiocese of Philadelphia make use of contemporary public relations techniques in order to promote the practice of the works of mercy—in this case the need to get warm clothing to those who need it for the upcoming bitterly cold Philadelphia winters. This is an excellent example of how the modern Church strives to carry out traditional practices using modern techniques and technology.

The rationale for maintaining a concern for doing what we can to get adequate clothing to those who need it goes beyond the obvious, however. The Gospel of Luke's narrative about John the Baptist includes the following:

> John said to the crowds that came out to be baptized by him, "You brood of vipers! Who warned you to flee from the wrath to come? Bear fruits worthy of repentance. Do not begin to say to yourselves, 'We have Abraham as our ancestor'; for I tell you, God is able from these stones to raise up children to Abraham. Even now the ax is lying at the root of the trees; every tree therefore that does not bear good fruit is cut down and thrown into the fire." And the crowds asked him, "What then should we do?" In reply he said to them, "Whoever has two coats must share with anyone who has none; and whoever has food must do likewise" (3:7–11).

In other words, the corporal work of mercy that directs us to "clothe the naked" isn't merely a pious directive. It's one expression of the basic dynamic at the heart of the gospel that is sometimes called "repentance," other times "conversion." In the Gospel of Mark, for example, Jesus announces the very heart of the gospel:

> Now after John was arrested, Jesus came to Galilee, proclaiming the good news of God, and saying, "The time is fulfilled, and the kingdom of God has come near; repent, and believe in the good news" (Mk 1:14–15).

One of the most basic ways authentic repentance and con-version of heart show themselves is by a readiness to share what we have with those who have much less. The extra coat in the closet belongs not to you but to someone who has no coat. The extra pair of shoes belongs not to you but to some-one who has no shoes. The basic issue is not one of mere "char-ity." Rather, the basic issue is one of justice.

It is unjust and unfair for anyone to have two coats as long as there is someone who has no coat at all. It is unjust and unfair for anyone to have two pairs of shoes as long as some-one has no shoes at all. This is the heart of the matter from the Christian point of view, and underlying this concern for jus-tice is the conviction that we are not isolated individuals but brothers and sisters of the same Father in heaven.

Does this mean that if you have two pairs of shoes, or two coats, that makes you less than a good Christian? There are radical Catholic social activists who might say yes. More likely, however, it means that you, like virtually all Christians, will never measure up perfectly to the ultimate ideals of the gospel. Also, it means that the society and culture we belong to some-times make demands on us that bring us into conflict with the gospel, and sometimes the culture wins. As long as we remain aware of the conflict, and of the culture winning, however, we can remain sensitive to the ideals we are called to attain and keep on trying to attain them, even if we never do. As long as we remain aware of the tension between the ideals and our inability to attain them, faith can remain alive and active.

To return to the point, however, the gospel imperative to "clothe the naked" isn't just an ethical "should" that tradition imposes on us. Rather, it is an expression of ongoing repen-tance and conversion of heart, one way that we turn away from self to focus on the needs of others. This spiritual dy-namic is the very heart of a life rooted in the gospel and guided by the Spirit of the risen Christ. Indeed, in a culture focused in many ways on superficialities this spiritual dynamic contributes to our freedom in ways of which we may not be aware.

The imperative to "clothe the naked" inspires us to do what we can, literally, to help provide clothing for those who need it. At the same time, it serves to remind us, as we mentioned previously, to be free from the demands of the fashion industry. There are many stories from the lives of the saints to provide added inspiration in this regard. While most of us can't imitate the saints literally, we can gather inspiration from them to maintain our own degree of freedom from the demands of "style" and "fashion." One of the most lovable examples of someone who lived out this spiritual imperative heroically was Saint Benedict Joseph Labré (1748–1783).

A religious vagrant, Benedict falls into the category of "holy fool for Christ." Early in his youth, Benedict decided to dedicate his whole life to God. Seeking to join the Trappists, they turned him away because he was too young. A whole stream of other religious communities likewise refused him entrance. Finally, Benedict decided that he was called to be a kind of holy derelict. He walked thousands of miles across Europe, praying and visiting shrines and churches. And here is where he is a particular inspiration for those who would maintain some freedom from the dictates of style and fashion: Benedict dressed in castoff clothes that were practically rags...and he never bathed!

Benedict seems to have avoided bathing in order to cultivate solitude for prayer—certainly one way to keep other people away. But the main point of his story is that Benedict Joseph Labré had no regard for what other people thought of how he dressed. Rather, his single-minded concern was love of God and neighbor. While his vocation was unique his priorities were not, for all Christians are called to place love at the heart of their lives, regardless of particular circumstances. If concern for dressing oneself and/or one's children fashionably becomes a preoccupation, or even a major concern, it can become an obstacle to love of God and neighbor. Concern for adequate clothing becomes a self-centered perversion instead of a corporal work of mercy. This may sound like an unlikely turn of events, but in a culture where movie stars and professional athletes become icons admired by the masses it's not such an extraordinary possibility.

The Letter of James, one of the less familiar gems among New Testament documents, makes it clear that concern for the basic needs of others is central to being a follower of Christ. At the same time, James makes clear the connection between the corporal works of mercy and authentic faith, insisting that to be real faith must express itself in works of mercy:

> What good is it, my brothers and sisters, if you say you have faith but do not have works? Can faith save you? If a brother or sister is naked and lacks daily food, and one of you says to them, "Go in peace; keep warm and eat your fill," and yet you do not supply their bodily needs, what is the good of that? So faith by itself, if it has no works, is dead. But someone will say, "You have faith and I have works." Show me your faith apart from your works, and I by my works will show you my faith. You believe that God is one; you do well. Even the demons believe—and shudder. Do you want to be shown, you senseless person, that faith apart from works is barren? Was not our ancestor Abraham justified by works when he offered his son Isaac on the altar? You see that faith was active along with his works, and faith was brought to completion by the works. Thus the scripture was fulfilled that says, "Abraham believed God, and it was reckoned to him as righteousness," and he was called the friend of God. You see that a person is justified by works and not by faith alone.

Likewise, was not Rahab the prostitute also justified by works when she welcomed the messengers and sent them out by another road? For just as the body without the spirit is dead, so faith without works is also dead (2:14–26).

This rather lengthy excerpt from the Letter of James makes it clear that getting adequate clothing to those who need it is more than just a nice gesture or an expression of Christian charity. Rather, "clothing the naked" is an action that authentic faith feels compelled to do because "faith without works is dead."

Another, perhaps startling "take" on this corporal work of mercy occurred when a woman in a medium-sized city in the Pacific Northwest felt called, as she said, to "do something about pornography and these strip joints." A Catholic—we'll call her Jane—she took to picketing "porn shops" and "strip joints." Two days a week, Jane carried her large, homemade sign as she walked up and down the sidewalk outside the porn shops and strip joints. Her sign read, "CLOTHE THE NAKED!"

While opposing pornography and strip joints isn't the most immediate meaning of this corporal work of mercy, you have to admire Jane's creativity and even her sense of humor. One day Jane decided that she would even go into a strip joint and "give witness" there. Taking with her a couple of long overcoats she bought at a Saint Vincent de Paul store, she went into a "nudie club" while a young woman was doing her "dance" routine, approached the stage, and began calling out, "Dear, please put this on. You poor thing! You must be chilly. You must be so embarrassed. Please! Do put this on!"

Jane was booed by the audience, of course, and the management quickly hustled Jane back out to the sidewalk. Jane returned to walking back and forth carrying her sign, but she decided to make her overcoat carrying incursion into "enemy territory," as she called it, a regular part of her "witness." So from then on, each time Jane went to "bear witness" she chose a strip club to enter, and the process would repeat itself. In she would go and begin calling out to the "dancer." Mere seconds later, back she would be on the sidewalk.

Soon, of course, the local media heard about Jane, and right away she became a celebrity. Many laughed at her. But Jane also attracted companions who began to accompany her in her "actions." Before long, a dozen men and women joined in, everyone walking up and down the street with signs two days a week. "Clothe the naked!" they would call out. Each time, several would also go with Jane into a strip club to offer overcoats to the strippers.

At first, the owners of the porn shops and strip clubs were amused. But after a few weeks, they began to get seriously irritated. They called the police who, by law, were obliged to instruct Jane and her group to remain outside on the sidewalks a certain distance away. They could not disrupt "business," or they would be arrested and taken to jail. Jane and her companions met to decide what they would do next. Were they willing to spend time in jail in support of their cause?

Since none of the antipornography activists were able to sacrifice time from work and families to go to jail, Jane's group decided instead to branch out. They formed a local nonprofit organization called "Clothe the Naked," complete with a board of directors and bylaws. The mission of the group was to continue twice-weekly picketing and educate the public about the damage done by the pornography industry.

Because Jane is Catholic, she could appreciate the double meaning of the corporal work of mercy from which her organization took its name. She could see the humor in it, but she could also see the perfectly serious purpose in the new meaning she gave to the old idea. She knew that both the old and new meanings of "clothe the naked" have to do with maintaining human dignity and helping people to maintain a more fully human standard of living.

Like all of the works of mercy, both corporal and spiritual, "to clothe the naked" lends itself to various understandings, and people will continue to find many ways to carry out this way of living out the mercy of Christ in this world.

CHAPTER 4

# To Visit the Imprisoned

Growing up in the 1950s and early 1960s, in the small southeastern Washington town of Walla Walla, I knew that on the outskirts of our town was the state penitentiary. The father of one of my friends from high school even worked there. But I never gave the prison much thought beyond wondering what it was like to work around all those "convicts." Even with all the emphasis on memorizing prayers and lists that came with using the *Baltimore Catechism*, I don't recall ever hearing anything about the implications of this fourth corporal work of mercy for we who lived right on the doorstep of a state prison.

We no doubt memorized the corporal works of mercy during the early grades at our Catholic elementary school. But we heard nothing more about what it might mean to actually live this particular work of mercy. Indeed, I looked at an old copy of the *Baltimore Catechism*, and sure enough, the answer to Question 191 is the seven corporal works of mercy. In my copy, this list is followed by a commentary, which begins on a no-nonsense note:

> Our Lord taught explicitly that one can earn the eternal reward of heaven by performing the corporal works

of mercy and that those who deliberately refuse to perform such works will be barred from heaven.[12]

Although the commentary doesn't say so, the apparent
scriptural reference is Matthew 25:31–46, the story of the sheep
and the goats. At any rate, the commentary that follows includes remarks about each of the corporal works of mercy,
with the exception of number 4, "To visit the imprisoned."
Perhaps the author of the commentary didn't know what to
say about this work of mercy that would make sense to his
young readers. Regardless, we never heard anything more about
it. Note, however, that we can't claim a great deal of progress
on this point. The *Catechism of the Catholic Church* (1994)
also, for whatever reason, offers no commentary on this particular corporal work of mercy....

This is a good example of a situation where sacred Tradition—which includes the corporal works of mercy—is more
in touch with the gospel than the catechetical authorities, of
the past or the present, were ready to cope with. It's clear that
in the Gospel of Matthew, Jesus advocates visiting those in
prison. Most likely, the second-century social and cultural situation in which Matthew's Gospel took shape and was finally
written down was one in which Christians could expect that
fellow believers would end up in the slammer in the normal
course of events. Therefore, it was obvious that they would be
called upon by their faith to visit those who were in prison.
Being Christian was a good way to get yourself thrown into
jail, and the mercy of Christ would require those not behind
bars to bring comfort and encouragement to those who were.

What this business of visiting those in prison would mean
for later generations of Christians is another matter, however.
For all but the first few centuries of Christian history, being a
Christian has been not only legal but, eventually, the socially
acceptable thing to be. Whereas the early Christians took it

for granted that you could be incarcerated for being a Christian, subsequent generations of believers took it for granted that if you were behind bars you deserved to be there. In other words, if you were put in jail it was, in effect, for doing something contrary to what it means to be "a good Christian." In other words, the reason for being in prison did a complete reversal!

This may be why we find a commentary on this corporal work of mercy in neither the old *Baltimore Catechism* nor the contemporary *Catechism of the Catholic Church*. Both may assume that to visit those who are imprisoned would be a simple gesture of kindness or charity since the one in prison belongs there out of justice. In some cases this is no doubt true, but given certain events since the 1960s, up until the present, this assumption calls for further scrutiny. For the truth is that since the 1960s, and even before that, some Christians have found themselves in jail precisely for their choice to act on their Christian faith in ways that brought them into conflict with civil laws and civil authorities.

It takes only a little historical research to learn the stories of individual Catholics, such as Catholic Worker cofounder Dorothy Day, who spent time in jail because she stood up for the rights of immigrant farm workers or refused to cooperate with preparations for war. Among the most prominent Catholics who spent time in prison for actions they took in opposition to the war in Vietnam in the late 1960s and early 1970s were Daniel Berrigan, S.J., and his brother, Philip Berrigan, along with more than a few of their companions.

One of the most prominent sites of faith-based social protest is the School of the Americas (SOA), located at Fort Benning in Columbus, Georgia. The School of the Americas—in the late 1990s the name was changed to Western Hemisphere Institute for Security Cooperation (WHISC)—is the U.S. Army's Spanish-language facility established to train Latin American military personnel. Established in 1946, the school, along with the U.S. Air Force's Inter-American Air Forces Academy attracts the largest number of Latin American military students.

The Army's operations and maintenance account, which comes from U.S. taxpayers, of course, funds the school. Student tuition costs are covered mainly by grants through the International Military Education and Training and International Narcotics Control program.

WHISC has been questioned for years, as it trained many Latin American military personnel before and during the 1970s, the years of the "national security doctrine"—the civil war years in Central America—in which Latin American armies ruled or had major influence and were responsible for serious human rights violations. Training manuals used at WHISC and elsewhere from the early 1980s through 1991 recommended and taught techniques that violated human rights and democratic standards.

WHISC graduates continue to surface in news reports regarding both current human rights cases and new reports on past cases. Defenders of the school, however, argue that they do not teach abuse, and that today the curriculum includes human rights as a component of every class. They also argue that no school should be held accountable for the actions of only some of its graduates. Nevertheless, each year protests are held at WHISC, and each year some of the protesters end up behind bars.

The point is that we live in an era when faith sometimes leads people into a situation not unlike that of the early Christians, where there is a conflict between faith and the secular institutions and laws. This means that the idea of visiting those in prison can be more today than a simple act of charity; it can be a way to support the faith of those whose faith leads them to sacrifice their liberty for the sake of higher values.

The idea of visiting the imprisoned is further complicated

today by the possibility that there may be social and economic injustices that contribute to the reasons some people are imprisoned. Is it a mere coincidence that most of those in prison today are nonwhite, poor, and underprivileged? To visit those who are in prison leads some to work for social and economic changes that would alleviate the causes of incarceration in the first place. It's fine to visit the imprisoned, but if those behind bars are there, in part at least, for reasons beyond their control, those who do the "visiting" may find themselves called to do something about those contributing unjust causes. Consider the following:

> The number of people in prison, in jail, on parole, and on probation in the U.S. increased threefold between 1980 and 2000, to more than 6 million, and the number of people in prison increased from 319,598 to almost 2 million in the same period. This buildup has targeted the poor, and especially Blacks. In 1999, though Blacks were only 13 percent of the U.S. population, they were half of all prison inmates. In 2000, one out of three young Black men was either locked up, on probation, or on parole. The military-industrial complex of the 1950s, with its Cold War communist bogeyman, has been replaced by a prison-industrial complex, with young Black "predators" serving as its justification.[13]

Suddenly, the corporal work of mercy "to visit the imprisoned" becomes something not so simple at all. This corporal work of mercy originated with the simple need to visit those imprisoned for their faith. Today, there are certainly places in the world where people are in prison for acting on their Christian faith, but most of the readers of this book live in places where this is unlikely to be the case. Rather, people are in prison, most likely, because they were convicted by the justice system of anything from drug violations to murder; from so-called "white collar crimes" to breaking and entering and dozens of other ways that people end up behind bars today. And, as the above quotation suggests, in more than a few instances social and economic conditions have as much, or more, to do with why people are in prison as their own choices and behavior.

All this has consequences for those who would practice the corporal work of mercy under consideration here. It means that most likely the option of simply going to the local jail to "visit" those incarcerated simply isn't an option. Just try calling the nearest county jail to inform whoever answers the phone that you want to show up there, say, once a week to "visit" one of the men or women in jail as a gesture of good will and concern for an unfortunate individual. If the person on the other end of the phone line doesn't laugh you off the face of the earth you'll be told to stop being so naive.

If, however, you were allowed to visit someone in jail you would soon find yourself coping with all kinds of issues you never imagined before. The person you are assigned to visit might easily try to take advantage of you, ask you to smuggle to him or her all kinds of things not allowed in the jail, or try to get you to give him or her money. If the person is jailed for a relatively short time, you could find yourself with a major nuisance on your hands, at the very least, when he or she is released from jail. The former inmate could take advantage of you in all kinds of ways after his or her jail time is over. It doesn't take much imagination to realize what this could lead to for you.

If you begin to take seriously the complex social and economic issues that lead to the huge prison populations we have today, first it could make your head spin; then, you could find yourself wondering about how on earth anyone could possibly act when it comes to "visiting the imprisoned." Unless you are the relative of someone in prison, you need to get a special security clearance to visit the imprisoned today. Then you need to have special training. Then you need to be part of a special program designed to serve specific needs of the men or women who are imprisoned. And so on and so forth. It can get very complicated! Of course, some people will do precisely this, those who have a special inclination or calling to be involved in prison ministries. But for most of us the possibility of actually visiting the imprisoned is remote.

If, however, we take seriously the idea that there is more than one way to be imprisoned, it becomes more likely we can think of ways to "visit the imprisoned" that don't require us to visit an actual correctional facility or prison. Think for a moment about ways people can be confined and their freedom severely restricted. The numbers of people today who are "imprisoned" by addictions of various sorts has taken on epidemic proportions. Think of the many people right in your own community who are confined to their homes or institutional facilities. It's easy to give time regularly to visiting people who are "imprisoned" in ways like these.

At the same time, if we use a little imagination we can think of ways people are imprisoned that have nothing to do with addictions or with being confined. Writer John Scott Shepherd's novel, *Henry's List of Wrongs*, tells the story of Henry Chase.[14] Nicknamed "the Assassin," he will do virtually anything to become rich and powerful, including conquests both in the business world and in the bedroom. There's not a glimmer left of human warmth and compassion in Henry's heart; he seems not to have a soul at all. Then, one night, his conscience comes back to haunt him.

With the help of a mysterious young woman named Sophie (from the Greek *sophia*, wisdom), Henry confesses that he has a heart of cold, hard stone:

"Please." He felt tears running down his face. He was drunk and afraid and suddenly very, very alone. She was almost to the door, now, groping behind her for the knob. He dropped to his knees and said it again: "Please. You have no idea." But it choked out in a sob. He was breaking down, holding himself, rocking. He closed his eyes tightly. When he opened them again, she'd pared the distance between them in half. "What have you done?" she asked.

He took a deep, shaking breath, like a child after a spanking. "Terrible things. I've hurt a lot of people."[15]

Henry Chase is a good fictional example of someone imprisoned in his own greed, self-centeredness, and lack of empathy and compassion for other people. For years, his sole focus has been on becoming as wealthy and powerful as possible. Then, unannounced, into his life comes Sophie Reilly, hotel maid. Since this is fiction, we are well advised to look for metaphors, and in fact Sophie is a metaphor for God, or at least the grace of God in the life of Henry Chase.

Sophie asks Henry to make a list of all the people he has hurt the most, then she accompanies him as he goes to see each of these people to ask their forgiveness. This is the only way Henry can find release from the prison of his own making he dwells in. Sophie, in other words, provides a good example of a way in which someone "visits the imprisoned" and not only "visits" but helps the other to achieve liberation.

Of course, few situations in real life are likely to be as dramatic as the one that constitutes the story of Henry Chase and Sophie Reilly. All the same, no one should ever minimize the value of simply listening sympathetically when someone wants to talk about past mistakes or choices. It can be spiritually and emotionally liberating when another person merely listens and tries to understand. Indeed, far more people are "imprisoned" by their past than are confined behind literal bars.

A real-life example of someone who understands the power of the gospel to liberate people in both literal and figurative prisons is Father Michael Kennedy, a Jesuit priest in East Los Angeles. Thinking creatively, Father Kennedy developed a way to use meditation and guided visualization to help people enter into stories from the gospels. In this way he helps change the lives of prisoners in a maximum-security prison, at-risk young people, ex-gang members, and refugees. Unwilling to limit his efforts, however, Father Kennedy also brings his meditation and guided visualization methods to business people, bishops, and teachers.

"The goal of gospel meditation is to transform us within so that we can help transform our world," Father Kennedy wrote.[16] The meditations have proved especially effective in programs Father Kennedy maintains in the high-risk section of Los Angeles' juvenile hall and in programs and at California's Pelican Bay maximum-security state prison, where he directs retreats for prisoners serving life sentences. Carrying messages about forgiveness, healing, and friendship, the meditations present an opportunity to be free from a culture of poverty and violence. By writing and using his meditations, Father Kennedy lives in a particularly creative way the corporal work of mercy "to visit the imprisoned."

Finally, in one of the hundreds of poems he wrote, Trappist monk and author Thomas Merton (1915–1968) reflected— not without a twinkle in his eye—on the ways society sometimes "imprisons" people for reasons beyond their control. In this case, the subject is women. In his poem, *There Has to Be a Jail for Ladies*, Merton wrote:

There has to be a jail where ladies go
When they are poor, without nice things,
and with their hair down.
When their beauty is taken from them,
when their hearts are broken
There is a jail where they must go.
There has to be a jail for ladies, says the Government,
When they are ugly because they are wrong.
It is good for them to stay there a long time
Until the wrong is forgotten.
When no one wants to kiss them any more,
Or only wants to kiss them for money
And take their beauty away
It is right for the wrong to be unheard of for a long time
Until the ladies are not remembered.
But I remember one favorite song,
And you ladies may not have forgotten:
　　"Poor broken blossom, poor faded flower,"
　　　　says my song....[17]

Merton's poem is about the dominant culture's discomfort with women who do not measure up to certain basic standards of acceptability. The dominant culture would rather not acknowledge or look at such women because they do not look like the ideal; they are not beautiful in the ways that magazines, movies, and television prefer women to be beautiful. They are not "socially acceptable," so they find themselves ignored or they feel invisible. They live in the prison of cultural indifference or, worse, the prison of cultural distaste.

People live in many kinds of prisons, and the corporal work of mercy that encourages us to visit them can, and should, be applied in as many creative ways as possible. Just as people are imprisoned in many ways, so we can apply a creative spirit to "visit" them in many different ways.

## CHAPTER 5

# To Shelter the Homeless

The *Baltimore Catechism*'s commentary on the corporal and spiritual works of mercy is a response to the question, "What must we do to love God, our neighbor, and ourselves?" The current *Catechism of the Catholic Church*, on the other hand, sets forth its remarks on the works of mercy in the section on the seventh commandment ("You shall not steal")—a rather perplexing fact, but there you are. Either way, the need to help provide housing for those who would otherwise have none is a need that never seems to go away. Anyone who has ever experienced homelessness never forgets what it's like to have no place of one's own in the world.

There are various kinds of homelessness, of course. Refugees are perhaps the most homeless people in the world, for they are without both home and country. Sometimes those whose own lives are not, and never have been, touched by the experience of being a refugee give little thought to the magnitude of the refugee crisis in today's world.

In the years following the Second World War, the international community established an agency to protect and assist the world's refugees, the Office of the United Nations High Commissioner for Refugees (UNHCR). Although UNHCR was first established with a limited three-year mandate, the forced movement of people has become increasingly more complex since the immediate post-World War II era. Today, no continent, and barely any country, in the world is untouched by the global refugee crisis. At the beginning of 2000 an estimated fourteen million people were living as refugees, uprooted from their homes and forced to cross an international border. Nearly six million people were refugees in the Middle East, the vast majority of them Palestinian refugees—the world's largest and oldest refugee population; and there were more than three million refugees in Africa. In fact, every country on that continent has been affected by refugee movements.[18]

Huge though they are, the global refugee statistics conceal an even greater displacement crisis: that of the internally displaced, people who are forced to flee their homes, often for the same reasons as refugees—war, civil conflict, political strife, and gross human rights violations—but who remain within their own country, do not cross an international border, and hence are not eligible for protection under the same international system as refugees. There are an estimated thirty million internally displaced persons in the world, and the number may be even higher. The largest internally displaced population is in Sudan, where four million people have been uprooted by the civil war that has gripped the country since about 1980; an estimated 2.5 million people have been displaced by civil conflict in Angola; 1.6 million people are displaced by conflict and human rights abuse in the Democratic Republic of the Congo; and 1.5 million people have been uprooted by the violence in Colombia.

Responses to the kinds of homelessness suffered by refugees tend to be shouldered by international aid organizations, and the average person can easily feel helpless when it comes to the suffering of so many people who seem to be so far away. But local churches and secular social-service agencies often sponsor refugee families who immigrate from distant lands,

and opportunities to help out with such activities are not difficult to come by. As necessary as such efforts are, of course, it is
important to take note of efforts to do something about
homelessness on the part of individuals.

In England, for example, a Catholic Housing Aid Society
worker, Susan Merl, wrote a play to be used in parish religious
education programs for children to highlight the plight of those
who have nowhere to call home. *Wherever You Go*, based on
the Old Testament Book of Ruth, uses speech, mime, movement, and music to tell the story of Ruth and Naomi who
search for somewhere to live and the response of a community
to their arrival.

Religious education coordinator, Carmel Martin, of Saint
John's Beaumont Preparatory School, in London, commented:
"Often biblical adaptations are of more value as entertainment than as a teaching tool, but Susan Merl has managed to
come up with something that engages with children, is easy to
use by teachers and remains faithful to the detail of the Old
Testament story."[19]

Ideal for school or church groups, the play comes with a
CD accompaniment, written, arranged, and sung by a musi-
cian named Chris Sutton. England's Catholic Housing Aid
Society promotes the play for use each January on Homelessness
Sunday, a day for churches of all denominations to join in
worship to speak up for justice, and to commit themselves to
action for change.

Susan Merl's play is a good example of how efforts to shelter the homeless can be encouraged and supplemented by creative projects. In the realm of direct action, however, one of
the most successful and most creative efforts to shelter the
homeless comes from the now widely recognized organization
Habitat for Humanity International. The story of the founders
of Habitat is the story of a married couple who decided to
make a life project of helping to shelter the homeless.

Millard and Linda Fuller are the cofounders of Habitat for Humanity International, a Christian organization dedicated to the elimination of homelessness and inadequate housing wherever in the world they exist. Habitat uses donated money and materials, together with volunteer labor to build or renovate houses which are then sold at cost to needy families that pay for them with mortgages that are interest free.

With Millard Fuller as president and Linda Fuller as virtual copresident, Habitat has witnessed phenomenal growth. In the first decade and a half of its existence, between 1976 and 1991, Habitat built an astonishing ten thousand houses in the United States and in other countries. This success was, however, only the beginning. It took Habitat just two more years to match that record by building another ten thousand homes. Then, only fourteen months later, Habitat built yet another ten thousand homes. As of 2002, Habitat had built more than one hundred thousand homes for families in more than fourteen hundred U.S. cities and fifty-six countries. It is now the seventeenth largest homebuilder in the U.S., putting up some forty-five thousand houses in 1998. Habitat for Humanity International builds a minimum of one house every hour of every day somewhere in the world.

If Millard and Linda Fuller were Catholics, they would be on the fast track toward becoming the first modern married couple to be considered for canonization as saints. Millard Fuller was born on January 3, 1935, in town of Lanett, Alabama. Millard's mother died when he was three years old, and the boy formed a particularly strong bond with his father who taught him how the world works. When he was only six years old, Millard Fuller earned a profit from raising a pig under his father's guidance.

Millard earned an undergraduate degree at Auburn University, then he completed studies at the University of Alabama Law School. After graduation in 1959, he and Linda Caldwell were married. Rather than practice law following graduation, Millard Fuller, together with fellow law school student Morris Dees, began a company, Fuller & Dees. By 1964, the success of this company led to both men becoming enormously wealthy. Millard and Linda Fuller enjoyed a life of comfort and luxury. However, as the business flourished the Fullers' marriage did not.

Desperate to heal their marriage, Linda Fuller separated from her husband in late 1964 and got some counseling from a minister in New York. Millard Fuller joined his wife there and, after a week of honest soul-searching, they reconciled, agreeing to begin their marriage again based on the Christian values they had grown up with.

At this key turning point in their lives, Millard and Linda decided to give up the business to which Millard Fuller had devoted himself. The Fullers sold their interest in the business, and they sold all of their material possessions and donated all the money to various Christian causes.

The virtually penniless couple then began to search for their mission in life. At one point they heard about Koinonia, a Christian commune led by Bible scholar Clarence Jordan. Koinonia was organized in 1942 under the Christian principles of nonviolence, racial equality and a common sharing of material goods. What had been planned as an overnight stay turned into a month, and the Fullers embraced this new, simple lifestyle. Although Millard and Linda left Koinonia at the end of the month, they eventually returned to apply their business and leadership skills to Clarence Jordan's creative ideas for helping others. The Fullers' adaptation of Jordan's concept for providing adequate housing for poor people would ultimately give birth to Habitat for Humanity International.

For the next several years, the Fullers worked at raising money for church supported schools and activities. During this time, they visited schools, hospitals, and agricultural projects in several African nations as missionaries of the church.

Returning to Koinonia in 1968, together with Clarence Jordan they began several partnership enterprises including a nonprofit ministry that would build housing for needy people. Beginning in 1969, the Fullers learned the business principles of homebuilding by participating in the construction of nearly thirty houses for needy people on the Koinonia site.

Millard and Linda Fuller returned to Africa in 1973 and applied their housebuilding skills there. With a $3,000 grant from the Koinonia community, they founded a program to construct small, cement-block houses for the poorest of the poor. Although the houses had no electricity or running water, they proved to be far better than the hovels in which the owners were previously living. During the three years the Fullers lived in Zaire, they built 114 houses. The success of the program became a working model for that developing nation to follow.

The Fullers also established in Zaire several other programs to assist the needy. Their "Rise Up and Walk" project raised funds for the purchase of artificial limbs for those with prosthetic needs. They also launched a program to collect unused eyeglasses from churches in the United States and distribute them at minimal cost to those in need in Zaire. Proceeds from the sales were used to finance the construction of still more homes.

The Fullers were convinced that their housing model could be adapted and extended to meet similar needs all over the world. Returning to Koinonia Farms in 1976, they began work on creating a new, independent organization, Habitat for Humanity International. Their model called for the establishment of affiliate groups anyplace in the world. Each group would be locally financed and responsible for developing housing projects appropriate to local conditions and needs.

Habitat's success received national prominence and support when, in 1984, former President Jimmy Carter and his wife, Rosalynn Carter, participated in their first Habitat work project. The Carters' personal involvement in Habitat's ministry brought national visibility to the organization and sparked interest in Habitat's work across the U.S. Habitat experienced a dramatic increase in the number of new affiliates around the country.

The Fullers live a life of modest means in a low-income neighborhood of Americus, Georgia. Their home, which has no air conditioning, was purchased for $12,400 nearly twenty years ago. They receive small salaries from Habitat, and both feel that they get everything they want from living a life based on Christian values. Thus, they consider themselves rich in ways not to be had from the accumulation of material possessions.

Millard and Linda Fuller coauthored *The Excitement Is Building*, a chronicle of Habitat for Humanity's success, and Millard Fuller has written a number of other books about Habitat for Humanity. Those books include: *A Simple, Decent Place to Live*, *The Theology of the Hammer*, *No More Shacks!*, *Love in the Mortar Joints*, and *Bokotola*. Linda Fuller is editor of Habitat's "Partners in the Kitchen" cookbook series which includes the titles *From Our House to Your's* and *Home Sweet Habitat*.

Both Millard and Linda Fuller have received many awards for their remarkable work including the 1994 Harry S. Truman Public Service Award. Millard Fuller received the Medal of Freedom from President Clinton in September 1996, was named Builder of the Year in 1995 by *Professional Builder* magazine, and received the Martin Luther King, Jr., Humanitarian Award from both the state of Georgia and the King Center.

Millard and Linda Fuller continue to spend virtually all of their time engaged in fund-raising, publicity, and other activities on behalf of Habitat for Humanity. Their faith, dynamism, and entrepreneurial spirit have led them to make dramatic advances toward their goal of eliminating poverty housing throughout the world. Millard Fuller expresses well both his and Linda's goals and the goals of Habitat for Humanity International: "We must put faith and love into action to make them real, to make them come alive for people."[20]

Without question, the story of Habitat for Humanity International is one of the biggest success stories ever when it comes to true stories about people who have put into practice the traditional Catholic corporal work of mercy which is the focus of this chapter. The fact that the story was and is being lived out by a Protestant married couple can only leave Catholics to ponder the extent to which Catholics have taken seriously the call of the gospel. Can anyone think of a Catholic, much less a Catholic married couple, who in recent memory sold all they had, gave the money to the poor, adopted an extremely simple lifestyle, and dedicated the rest of their lives to serving the poor in some way? One can only wonder about the extent to which most Catholics actually take to heart the deepest meanings of their religious tradition as the Catholic Church, the church that traces its roots directly to the apostles of Christ, and through them to Jesus himself, moves into the twenty-first century.

The corporal work of mercy called "shelter the homeless" does not point us in some vague direction; neither is it a mere pious platitude or simpleminded point for meditation. Rather, the fact that "to shelter the homeless" appears in this list of the works of mercy should make it clear to all that among the conditions a loving God most abhors is the condition of homelessness. As far as the Father of Jesus is concerned, as long as anyone is homeless those who have homes are obliged to do something about it. This is not a matter of "if you feel like it" or "if you're so inclined." Rather, we have no choice, if our faith is authentic, but to make whatever personal and financial sacrifices are necessary in order to shelter those who have no homes.

This is a nitty-gritty issue, no question about that. At the same time, we can, and may, benefit from reflection on various ways this issue has meaning. First of all, of course, it has meaning because of the human need for shelter. No one should ever be without four walls around them, a roof over their head, and the basic necessities of modern life including indoor plumbing, electricity, and so forth. But we should not overlook the religious and spiritual meaning of having a home, as well. From the Christian perspective, indeed, to have a home is to not only have a place of shelter in the world but to experience the presence of God. Consider some rarely read words from the New Testament's Book of Revelation:

> And I heard a loud voice from the throne saying, "See, the home of God is among mortals. He will dwell with them as their God; they will be his peoples, and God himself will be with them…" (21:3).

The author of Revelation uses "home" in a tremendously powerful way, but his use of this word depends upon the experience of the reader for its power. Readers who know what it is to have a "home" can grasp the deeper meaning when Revelation says that "the home of God is among mortals." At the same time, however, anyone who has had a home and then lost it may find these words even more meaningful. The idea that God, the Creator of the universe, the Father of Jesus and Father to all who are "in Christ," would make his home not in some distant heaven but in the midst of "mortals"—so that, in fact, heaven is no longer distant but in our midst—is an expression of divine love to boggle the imagination.

There is no question that the most important responses we can make to homelessness are those that provide adequate shelter to those who have no home to live in. But it remains true, also, that insights we can gain from these words in Revelation remain valid. In other words, there is such a reality as spiritual homelessness, too. To be unaware of or alienated from God is to experience a kind of homelessness that can afflict even the most comfortable and the most affluent. People living in the grandest houses can suffer from the homelessness that results from having no ongoing experience of God's loving presence in their lives.

Therefore, there is a connection between this corporal work of mercy called "to shelter the homeless" and various forms of pre-evangelization, evangelization, and catechesis. For one of the primary objectives of proclaiming and teaching the gospel is to bring those with no awareness and/or experience of God's love to just such an experience. The goal is to help people to "come home" in the fullest spiritual and human sense.

Indeed, this spiritual form of homelessness is most widespread in the more affluent countries, the so-called "developed" nations of the earth. It almost seems that spiritual homelessness is directly proportional to the level of material comfort people have. Quite often, those who visit a place where the people are poor in material terms return to their comfortable homes almost literally "blown away" by the joy they found in the lives of the "poor" they visited.

CHAPTER 6

# To Visit the Sick

The Book of Sirach says: "Do not hesitate to visit the sick, because for such deeds you will be loved" (7:35). This quotation expresses the obvious notion that it is a "work of mercy" to visit people who are sick. For the essence of mercy is empathy and compassion, and who experiences this more than someone who receives a visit when they are laid low by sickness? Indeed, if there is a corporal work of mercy that we tend to practice without even thinking about it this would be the one. When someone we know—it doesn't even need to be someone we love dearly—is sick, especially if their affliction is serious enough to put them in the hospital—our natural response is to visit, to "cheer up" the one who is hospitalized.

The most immediate source of Christian dedication to this particular corporal work of mercy is the words of Jesus in Matthew 25 ("I was sick and you took care of me"). Still, by including this work of mercy in his story, Jesus simply showed his Jewishness and taught his disciples to remain rooted in this strand of Jewish tradition. Indeed, down through the centuries Judaism has preserved this dedication to visiting the sick, as we can see in the following excerpts from a commentary on the Talmud:

Rabbi Johanan once fell ill and Rabbi Hanina went in to visit him. He said to him: Are your sufferings welcome to you? He replied: Neither they nor their reward. He said to him: Give me your hand. He gave him his hand and he raised him. Why could not Rabbi Johanan raise himself? They replied: The prisoner cannot free himself from jail (Talmud, Berachot 5b).

Rabbi Helbo is sick. But none visited him. He rebuked them [the scholars], saying, "Did it not once happen that one of Rabbi Akiba's disciples fell sick, and the Sages did not visit him? So Rabbi Akiba himself entered [his house] to visit him, and because they swept and sprinkled the ground before him, he recovered. "My master," said he, "you have revived me!" [Straightway] Rabbi Akiba went forth and lectured: He who does not visit the sick is like a shedder of blood (Talmud, Nedarim 40a).

He who visits the sick causes him to live, whilst he who does not causes him to die (Talmud, Nedarim 40a).

Rab said: He who visits the sick will be delivered from the punishments of Gehenna, for it is written, Blessed is he that considereth the poor: the Lord will deliver him in the day of evil. "The poor"…means none but the sick, as it is written, He will cut me off from pining sickness… (Talmud, Nedarim 40a).

Rabbi Shisha son of Rabbi Idi said: One should not visit the sick during the first three or the last three hours [of the day], lest he thereby omit to pray for him. During the first three hours of the day his [the invalid's] illness is alleviated; in the last three hours his sickness is most virulent (Talmud, Nedarim 40a).

Rabbi Abba son of Rabbi Hanina said: He who visits
the sick takes away a sixtieth of his pain (Talmud,
Nedarim 39b).

We have to not only take care of ourselves; we also have to
take care of one another. We all have moments when we need
to depend on others for our well being, and we all have the
opportunity to be a help to those who have helped us. The
sages of the Talmud went into great detail regarding why one
should visit the sick, when you should visit, and how you can
best be a help and not a hindrance. The *mitzvah* (commandment) of visiting the sick is one of those that brings out the
best in humanity.[21]

There is an account of a particularly notable situation in a
biography of Bill Monroe, "the father of bluegrass music."[22]
On March 15, 1996, the eighty-four-year-old Monroe hosted
two consecutive fifteen-minute segments of the legendary Grand
Ole Opry, near Nashville, Tennessee. That night, Bill felt particularly tired, and the next day he was disoriented. A friend
rushed him to a Nashville hospital where it was determined
that Bill had suffered a stroke.

Many people visited Bill Monroe in the hospital. During
the visit of one friend, Bill began to weep. "He turned his face
to the wall to hide his tears," wrote biographer Richard D.
Smith.[23] "'I didn't know until I was sick that people cared for
me as much as they do,' he said."[24]

Another friend and associate, Tony Conway, had Bill's
valuable mandolin for safekeeping. "Now he visited Bill in the
hospital, put it into his hands, and gave him a pick. Monroe
regarded the instrument slowly and strummed it lightly. Suddenly, he kicked into a rousing instrumental that Tony had
never heard, evidently a new composition. The he sang 'Blue
Moon of Kentucky.'"[25]

Later, Conway brought Bill a brand-new Gibson mandolin

that the company had given Bill as part of an endorsement deal. He advised the medical staff caring for Bill to let him play it as therapy. When another entertainer, Marty Stuart, accompanied Tony Conway to see Bill, the two men found Monroe unresponsive. "I know why you can't play that mandolin," Stuart said cheerfully. "You don't have your hat on."[26]

Marty found Monroe's Stetson hat and kindly placed it on the old man's balding head. "Sure enough, Monroe came to life. He tore into [a tune called] 'Wheel Hoss,' and Stuart was soon playing a spirited duet with his idol. Then Bill tipped his hat and took a little bow. Just like he'd do onstage."[27]

Monroe's condition deteriorated, however, and he was moved first to another hospital, then to a care center in Springfield, about twenty-five miles north of Nashville. Although he had often been standoffish in his lifetime, in his later years Bill often said, "We should all be friends." During these final days, his many friends gathered to support Bill in his final illness. Often they would play their instruments and sing for Bill, and he would open his eyes and whisper, "That's fine, that's powerful."[28] When someone sang, "Jesus Loves Me" for Bill he put his hands together in prayer, his fingertips touching under his chin, in the way he always prayed."[29]

Finally, at 1:20 P.M., on Monday, September 9, 1996, Bill Monroe passed from this world.[30] The point of this narrative, however, is to illustrate the goodness of a gesture that we often take for granted, the simple gesture of visiting the sick. Sometimes we take this for granted, so naturally does it come to us. We may minimize its importance. In fact, however, it can make such a big difference and have such a positive effect on those who are sick that we should never underestimate its value.

Few people who are sick are major figures in the world of music or entertainment, however, and few of us will ever be in a position to visit such people when they are sick. Not only that, but visiting the sick can be one of the simplest ways to build into one's life a focus on the needs of others, to grow in unselfishness and in disregard for oneself. Virtually anyone can find ways to visit the sick, and it doesn't require any special qualifications.

When Jack turned sixty-five he retired from what he called "the world of work for pay." During the months prior to his retirement, Jack thought about what he wanted to do with his time once he no longer had to leave home each day to go to work. Over the years he had developed an interest in model railroads, but he knew he wouldn't want to spend more than a few hours a week on this hobby. Later in life he also began to take piano lessons, so he knew he would want to practice every day. But Jack had also started taking his Catholic faith more seriously in the last fifteen years or so, and he had done more reading in his spare time in order to understand his faith better.

Finally, Jack decided that he would volunteer two mornings per week at a local nursing home. As it turned out, he not only spent his time visiting with the residents of the nursing home, but when the staff discovered that Jack played the piano they asked him to include some time at the piano in the recreation room each morning he was there. Jack was no Horowitz, but everyone enjoyed the simple tunes he played, and for Jack it was extra practice time he appreciated having. At home, he began working up new tunes to play at the nursing home, so that gave him more motivation to improve his piano skills.

Jack enjoyed playing the piano for the nursing home's residents, but even more he liked simply going from room to room to spend time with those who were unable to leave their beds. With those who wanted to talk, he worked at being a good listener. With the less talkative he often asked if they would like him to read aloud to them, and he was surprised at how often the idea received an affirmative response. Jack read books, both fiction and nonfiction, he read magazine articles, and he read from the daily newspaper or from news magazines. Sometimes this would lead to discussions.

"It's such a simple thing," Jack comments, "this 'visiting the sick.' Anyone, really, can do it. All it takes is time and the willingness to listen and share yourself. You would be amazed at how many people in retirement communities and nursing homes die more from loneliness than any real physical affliction. Sometimes I think the physical afflictions actually come from, or get worse because of, being lonely."

Another avid practitioner of the corporal work of mercy called "to visit the sick" is Lenore, a woman in her early seventies. The people in the nursing homes and retirement centers where Lenore spends much of her time call her "the banjo lady" because she always brings along her five-string banjo to play and sometimes sing. "Mostly I just play simple tunes," Lenore explains. "I'm no banjo virtuoso. When I was in my early fifties I decided that I wanted to learn to play the five-string banjo. I had always loved the sound, my kids were grown and gone, and I just decided to go ahead and do it. After a few years, when I got involved in going around to the nursing homes, convalescent centers, and then the retirement communities, I started bringing my banjo with me, and everyone loved it, even though I still play at a fairly rudimentary level. The darn thing weighs about twelve pounds, so I get good exercise myself just from lugging it around," she declares with a laugh.

Lenore's husband died a couple of years ago, and that left her with even more time to "visit the sick." Four days a week, she puts her banjo into the back seat of her car, then she drives around to four or five different places where she talks with the residents—many of whom are not much older than she is— listens, laughs, commiserates, and plays her banjo. Now and then she gives an informal presentation she put together called "Introducing the Five-String Banjo."

"Where I live the banjo is uncommon," Lenore explains. "Not many people have actually seen a banjo up close. So I talk about the history of the banjo, where it came from and how it's really the only truly American musical instrument that really caught on. I explain about the various parts of the banjo and how it's put together. Then I explain about the different kinds of banjo and the different styles of playing. I answer questions, then I play a few tunes. People really seem to enjoy it. Sometimes the nursing homes and so forth insist on paying me a little something for my effort, so I use that money to pay for gas and banjo strings."

Lenore plans to go on visiting the sick for as long as she can. "It keeps me active, you know, so I guess I'll keep at it for as long as I can drive and still get the ol' banjo out of its case. I suppose I'll move to a retirement center myself someday, but then I'll just have a captive audience for my visiting and playing. I'll probably drive them all nuts!"

In the New Testament's Letter of James we find these words: "Are any among you sick? They should call for the elders of the church and have them pray over them, anointing them with oil in the name of the Lord" (5:14). When it comes to "visiting the sick" Catholicism isn't satisfied with just visiting. When people are, in one way or another, seriously ill we have a sacrament, the anointing of the sick, to share with them. Recall that any of the seven sacraments is a visible sign of an invisible reality, the real presence of the risen Christ given to us in ways we can perceive with our senses. The *Catechism of the Catholic Church* says about this sacrament: "The proper effects of the sacrament include a special grace of healing and comfort to the Christian who is suffering the infirmities of serious illness or old age, and the forgiving of the person's sins."[31]

Clara recently celebrated her eightieth birthday. She is fortunate enough to still be quite active and still living independently in her own home, and her health is good, too. "Just lucky, I guess," she says with a smile. Still, whenever her parish schedules a communal celebration of the sacrament of anointing the sick, Clara participates. "It's quite nice," she explains. "I always feel better, even physically, for days after I receive the anointing of the sick. I'm not really 'sick-sick,' but I am eighty years old, after all, so with that comes plenty of aches and pains, stiffness of the joints, that sort of thing. I get around fine, but the anointing of the sick seems to have this marvelous effect of both relieving the aches and pains and nourishing me spiritually so I don't feel like complaining so much about life's woes in general."

Clara's pastor, Father Mark, speaks from his own experience as a minister of the sacrament of anointing the sick. "As a parish priest, I probably do more 'visiting the sick' than most people. I visit parishioners in the hospital two days a week and whenever an emergency comes up. I enjoy the visiting, of course, but I find that whenever I offer the sacrament of anointing people appreciate that. Older people sometimes still think of this as 'Extreme Unction,' the old understanding of the sacrament that limited it to people on death's doorstep, so I need to help them understand that this isn't what I'm offering, which they are usually relieved to hear. But once we get beyond that, the sacrament of anointing the sick is a real source of comfort and healing. It makes 'visiting the sick' an even deeper and more spiritually rewarding experience—for them *and* for me."

That visiting the sick is so readily available as a way for just about anyone to reach out to and care for others should not, however, mask the fact that there are some basic skills needed in order to practice this particular corporal work of mercy. These skills can be summarized concisely by Elizabeth Menkin, M.D. She puts it this way:

Be there.

Be quiet. (Listen)

It's not about you. (Don't direct the conversation to your own problems, or be so hung up on your own discomfort with the situation that you cannot be present.)

Bottom line: Show up and shut up![32]

Let's take a closer look at each of these skills for visiting the sick.

*Be there.* This is at once the easiest and the most difficult skill. First, we need to make the time and expend the energy to get to where the sick person is. This may sound easier than it is. It means that you need to leave behind all the other ways you can be using your time. Your work, your leisure activities, your distractions, the television programs you could be watching, the other people you could be with. You need to leave all these behind and go to where the sick person is. Chances are this will not be as pleasant a situation as the one you leave behind. You can probably count on the fact that it won't be as enjoyable as dozens of other things you can think of to do.

Once you get to where the sick person is, the challenges are not behind you. One you're there, the challenge is to really *be there*. The challenge is to really *be present* to the sick person. Don't start to leave, mentally, almost as soon as you arrive. Instead, try to be there and be open. Don't arrive with an agenda of your own. Which leads to the next skill for visiting the sick.

*Be quiet. (Listen.)* Chances are, the sick person isn't anxious to have you do much more than simply be there and be ready to listen to him or her. You probably will only need to ask the occasional question or make a comment to draw the sick person into talking. Then, your job is to be quiet and listen, contributing only the occasional acknowledgment that you hear what he or she is saying. "That must be difficult." "I hear you."

*It's not about you.* Sometimes the inclination can be to turn the conversation toward what you want to talk about instead of what the sick person wants to talk about. Remember, you didn't come to make the sick person listen to your problems or woes. You're not there to fill in the sick person on what's going on in your life. You're there to be still and listen.

*Bottom line: Show up and shut up!* This says it all in a nutshell. If you can get yourself into the presence of the sick person, and if you can get yourself to zip your lips, then your visiting the sick will begin to have some value to the sick person. The goal is to be there for the sick person—not for yourself.

CHAPTER 7

# To Bury the Dead

The first six corporal works of mercy appear in the previously mentioned biblical parable of the sheep and the goats (Mt 25:31–46). According to the parable, those who have done these good deeds will go to heaven while those who have failed to do them will suffer eternal misery. As early as the third century the corporal work of mercy that is the subject of this chapter, to bury the dead, was added to bring the number up to seven. The burial of the dead was included because it is highly praised in the Book of Tobit:

> I would give my food to the hungry and my clothing to the naked; and if I saw the dead body of any of my people thrown out behind the wall of Nineveh, I would bury it. I also buried any whom King Sennacherib put to death when he came fleeing from Judea in those days of judgment that the king of heaven executed upon him because of his blasphemies. For in his anger he put to death many Israelites; but I would secretly remove the bodies and bury them. So when Sennacherib looked for them he could not find them (1:17–18).

Time was, this corporal work of mercy seemed to make more sense than it does today. Everyone must die, of course, but in the places where the readers of this book are likely to live, death has become removed from most people's experience as an everyday reality. Time was, when someone died members of the deceased person's own family prepared him or her for burial. Today, like so many other aspects of life, death is primarily the concern of professionals. Small-town Catholic undertaker and poet Thomas Lynch describes his work thus:

> Every year I bury a couple hundred of my townspeople. Another two or three dozen I take to the crematory to be burned. I sell caskets, burial vaults, and urns for the ashes. I have a sideline in headstones and monuments. I do flowers on commission.
>
> Apart from the tangibles, I sell the use of my building: eleven thousand square feet, furnished and fixtured with an abundance of pastel and chair rail and crown moldings. The whole lash-up is mortgaged and re-mortgaged well into the next century. My rolling stock includes a hearse, two Fleetwoods, and a minivan with darkened windows our price list calls a service vehicle and everyone in town calls the Dead Wagon.
>
> I used to use the *unit pricing method*—the old package deal. It meant that you had only one number to look at. It was a large number. Now everything is item-ized. It's the law. So now there is a long list of items and numbers and italicized disclaimers, something like a menu or the *Sears Roebuck Wish Book*, and some-times the federally mandated options begin to look like cruise control or rear-window defrost. I wear black most of the time, to keep folks in mind of the fact that we're not talking Buicks here. At the bottom of the list there is still a large number.

In a good year the gross is close to a million, 5 percent of which we hope to call profit. I am the only undertaker in this town. I have a corner on the market.

When we have professionals to bury the dead, what are we to do with this old corporal work of mercy that admonishes *us* to bury the dead? Are we forced to limit ourselves to interpreting this work of mercy as metaphor or apply it in figurative ways, as best we can? Perhaps. But there is another tack available to us. Modern medical science and healthcare extends life far beyond what our ancestors could expect. But frequently we find that one of the side "benefits" is that death, too, has become more of a "process." Instead of simply speaking of "death," now we often hear the phrase "death and dying." One way we can make more meaningful the work of mercy that is this chapter's subject is to shift its focus away from care for the body after death to care for the person who is dying.

One of the best-known organized forms of care for the dying is hospice. This program, which exists in many places, may be described thus:

- Hospice is a special concept of care designed to provide comfort and support to patients and their families when a life-limiting illness no longer responds to cure-oriented treatments.
- Hospice care neither prolongs life nor hastens death. Hospice staff and volunteers offer a specialized knowledge of medical care, including pain management.
- The goal of hospice care is to improve the quality of a patient's last days by offering comfort and dignity.
- Hospice care is provided by a team-oriented group of specially trained professionals, volunteers, and family members.
- Hospice addresses all symptoms of a disease, with a special emphasis on controlling a patient's pain and discomfort.

- Hospice deals with the emotional, social, and spiritual impact of the disease on the patient and the patient's family and friends.
- Hospice offers a variety of bereavement and counseling services to families before and after a patient's death.[33]

The word "hospice" comes from the Latin word *hospitium* meaning "guesthouse." Originally, this term was used to describe a place of shelter for exhausted and ill travelers returning from religious pilgrimages. During the 1960s an English physician, Dr. Cicely Saunders, began the modern hospice movement when he founded St. Christopher's Hospice near London. St. Christopher's organized a team approach to professional caregiving. It was the first program to use modern pain-management techniques to compassionately care for the dying. In 1974, the first hospice in the United States was established in New Haven, Connecticut.

As of this writing, there are more than 3,100 hospice programs in the United States including the U.S. territories of Puerto Rico and Guam. Hospice programs cared for nearly 540,000 people in the United States in 1998.

It is important to realize that hospice is not a place. The first hospice, at St. Christopher's in England, was established in a specific institutional setting, it's true. But in the intervening years hospice has come to refer to the kind of caregiving that hospice provides. Eighty percent of hospice care is provided in the homes of dying persons and in nursing homes. In some places, however, following the pattern of the original St. Christopher's hospice, inpatient units are available to assist with caregiving when home or nursing home resources are inadequate.[34]

Among those who can still take this work of mercy literally today are those responsible for Catholic cemeteries. Writing in *U.S. Catholic* magazine, Kathy Saunders explained that

Catholic cemetery personnel have a responsibility to bury the dead whether rich or poor.[35] Catholic cemeteries almost always make provision to provide burials for those who cannot afford the usual expenses. "And after a funeral," Saunders wrote, "Catholic cemetery personnel also have an obligation to walk with the bereaved on the long, painful process of healing. It's a mission that Catholic cemeteries accept with enthusiasm, according to Ellen Woodbury, past president of the National Catholic Cemetery Conference. Cemeteries, Woodbury says, are among the first organizations to develop support programs for grieving families." Saunders continues:

> Woodbury's Rockville Centre, New York, diocese sends a Mass card inviting families to the cemetery on the day their loved one is to be interred. And another personal note is usually sent a year later inviting them to return for an anniversary Mass. Retired diocesan priests often volunteer to deliver special homilies and provide comfort to mourners. Families of the deceased also are invited to attend gatherings at the cemetery on holy days and holidays.

In the Catholic Diocese of Brooklyn, since the mid 1950s the St. Vincent de Paul Society has been responsible for a program that provides free Christian burials for Catholics who can't afford to pay for them, for those who die with no family, and for deceased infants whose parents cannot pay for a funeral. "Many of those buried through this program not only have no one to bury them but also no one to pray for them," Kathy Saunders explains. "The society arranges for a priest to perform the funeral liturgy and its members continue to pray for all those who were buried through the program."

Saunders again quotes Ellen Woodbury, who dedicated many years ministering to bereaved families. Catholic cemetery workers are living examples of the mercy of the church toward the dead and their survivors.

> I believe that the burial of the dead and the reverence for their eternal remains is an integral part of my faith.
>
> In choosing this ministry as my career, I am following my religious belief in assisting those who need comfort, establishing trust funds for future care and maintenance, and providing, on a daily basis, for the reverent maintenance of the burial places of those who predeceased me, as part of my faith.

Clearly, since "to bury the dead" became the seventh and final corporal work of mercy our understanding of this way of being merciful has become much deeper and more inclusive. One of the more recent developments in the Catholic understanding of this work of mercy is the Church's acceptance of cremation as an alternative to burial.[36] We need to say, then, that to provide cremation for a deceased person's body can be just as much a work of mercy as providing burial. All the same, most of the development in our understanding of this work of mercy relates to the process of dying itself rather than to what we do with the body after death.

Sheila has been a hospice volunteer for three years, a form of service she undertook after extensive reading on the topic of death and dying and the dominant popular western culture's intense denial of death. Sheila explains: "I decided that to care for those who are dying would be a good way to be of service to others and, at the same time, to counter the cultural denial of death by facing it myself. People who are dying are among the most honest and caring people I've ever met. After doing this for three years I wouldn't give it up for anything."

Maggie, on the other hand, started out with no intention of becoming a hospice volunteer chaplain. A deacon from her

parish invited Maggie to accompany him to a training session
for hospice chaplains so she went along not knowing what it
was about. Once she realized what was going on she was "too
embarrassed to leave." As the training session progressed, however, Maggie began to realize that she wanted to do this—
"although with great fear and trepidation."

Ordinarily, only ordained clergy are allowed to become
hospice chaplains. But Maggie had recently completed a
master's degree in pastoral ministry, so they allowed her to
remain. Now she is the only nonordained chaplain in her area
doing spiritual work with dying persons.

Maggie says that the easiest part of her hospice work is
"being with people who are dying." At the same time, this is
also the most difficult part.

> Being with people spiritually and hearing their stories
> is wonderful, something I'm very grateful for. All the
> sensory stuff is most difficult—the smells and the whole
> setting the dying person must be in. Being one-on-one
> with people is good. You get to love a lot of people,
> really get to know them. After each one dies, of course,
> there is always a bereavement process. I need to take
> time off after that happens.

Maggie sometimes presides at funeral services. She finds
this most difficult when the family has no religious or spiritual
tradition on which to draw. At the same time, the family may
have a religious tradition but they refuse to connect with it at
the time of the loved one's death. "It's a major denial-of death
thing. They don't want any service, no ritual. At other times,
however, the dying person asks Maggie to help plan a funeral
service. The question she starts from is, 'What sort of celebration do you want to have for your life?'

"The most important thing," Maggie says, "is walking with

and being absolutely available to the dying person so they have the kind of death that's okay for them."

Funeral director Thomas Lynch, quoted earlier in this chapter, tells a marvelous story of a time when his profession required him to be caring and compassionate in ways related but prior to someone's actual death. The person was an old lady named Mary Jackson, an actress who had a recurring role on the old television series, "The Waltons." Mary spent half the year living in Hollywood and the other half living in her and Lynch's hometown of Milford, Michigan.

Mary Jackson was determined that she would be buried in Oak Grove Cemetery alongside all her relatives. She even had the route planned that the vehicle carrying her casket would take, and this required passing over the Oak Grove Bridge which spanned the Huron River. Then one day the bridge collapsed, and no plan was made to replace it. Neither the city nor the county could afford to repair or replace the bridge. Mary went to see Thomas Lynch, and she was outraged.

> She said she wanted to make her "arrangements." She brought a list of pallbearers and alternatives—stunt doubles she called them. She said I should read a poem—"The Hat-Weaver" by Edna St. Vincent Millay—and that the Methodist minister should do the rest. That she trusted me with the ultimate theater I took as high praise. Then she told me she had made a decision. She steadfastly refused to be buried by way of the back door of Oak Grove. In all of her eighty plus years, she explained, she had seen, in her mind's eye, the tasteful little procession leaving the funeral home by First Street, detouring slightly down Canal and right on Houghton, thus passing her house (the hearse pausing briefly according to custom), then left on Atlantic, right on Mont-Eagle, then down to the

river, crossing by the bridge under the high gate of Oak
Grove to rest in the companionable earth there. She
would not, she insisted, be a "spectacle," processing
down through town while strangers shopped in the
dime store or browsed in the sale racks of Arms Brothers or Dancers Fashions.[37]

Wanting to be as helpful as possible, Lynch suggested possibly using a raft of some sort to ferry across the river. "Never!"
Mary responded. "Not even over my dead body!"[38]
Not being aware that to have the old Oak Grove Bridge
repaired and returned to service was impossible, Mary teamed
up with Wilbur Johnson, a neighborly old guy from a local
grocery store, and eventually they accomplished the "impossible," and the old bridge was reborn. At the dedication cer-
emony, she read a poem that Thomas Lynch composed. Lynch
describes the scene:

And people stood among the stones and listened while
Mary's voice rose up over the river and mingled in the
air with the echo of Catholic bells tolling and tunes in
the Presbyterian steeple and the breeze with the first
inkling of June in it working in the fresh buds of winter oaks. The fire whistle was silent. No dogs howled.[39]

Indeed, the form that Thomas Lynch's service took, his
way in this instance to "bury the dead," was unique. He helped
Mary Jackson to know that the drive her mortal remains would
take to their final resting place would be the one she wanted, a
route not "defiled" by the world of buying and selling and the
hawking of commodities. It would be a passage through tree-
lined streets, and old homes, and over the river. This meant a
great deal to Mary, and Thomas Lynch did what he could to
help make it happen, even to encouraging Mary's own efforts

when he thought them as exercises in futility. And then he wrote a ceremonial poem for Mary to read when her dream came true. A unique form of service to help "bury the dead," but a real one all the same.

Finally, there are some words from the Gospel of Luke that we should not overlook:

> Now there was a good and righteous man named Joseph, who, though a member of the council, had not agreed to their plan and action. He came from the Jewish town of Arimathea, and he was waiting expectantly for the kingdom of God. This man went to Pilate and asked for the body of Jesus. Then he took it down, wrapped it in a linen cloth, and laid it in a rock-hewn tomb where no one had ever been laid. It was the day of Preparation, and the sabbath was beginning. The women who had come with him from Galilee followed, and they saw the tomb and how his body was laid. Then they returned, and prepared spices and ointments.
>
> On the sabbath they rested according to the commandment.
>
> But on the first day of the week, at early dawn, they came to the tomb, taking the spices that they had prepared. They found the stone rolled away from the tomb, but when they went in, they did not find the body. While they were perplexed about this, suddenly two men in dazzling clothes stood beside them. The women were terrified and bowed their faces to the ground, but the men said to them, "Why do you look for the living among the dead? He is not here, but has risen. Remember how he told you, while he was still in Galilee, that the Son of Man must be handed over to sinners, and be crucified, and on the third day rise again." Then they remembered his words, and returning from

the tomb, they told all this to the eleven and to all the
rest (23:50—24:9).

From the Christian faith perspective—that is, in the light
of our ongoing experience of the risen Christ in the midst of
the community of faith—we may never address this work of
mercy, this "burying the dead," without reminding ourselves
that any ministry to those who are dying, or to their mortal
remains following death, is a ministry which communicates
the spirit and reality of Christ's own Resurrection. For we truly
share in this Resurrection and in its power even here and now.
Indeed, "to bury the dead" is to proclaim our faith in—our
experience of—this Resurrection.

# The
# SPIRITUAL
# Works *of* Mercy

CHAPTER 8

# To Admonish the Sinner

The spiritual works of mercy, like the corporal works of mercy, find their source in Scripture and the practice of the Church since its earliest days. The first of these, "to admonish the sinner," may strike a jarring note with the modern ear, however, so we do well to make explicit the scriptural connections:

[Jesus said:] "If another member of the church sins against you, go and point out the fault when the two of you are alone. If the member listens to you, you have regained that one. But if you are not listened to, take one or two others along with you, so that every word may be confirmed by the evidence of two or three witnesses. If the member refuses to listen to them, tell it to the church; and if the offender refuses to listen even to the church, let such a one be to you as a Gentile and a tax collector" (Mt 18:15–20).

But we appeal to you, brothers and sisters, to respect those who labor among you, and have charge of you in the Lord and admonish you; esteem them very highly in love because of their work. Be at peace among yourselves. And we urge you, beloved, to admonish the

idlers, encourage the fainthearted, help the weak, be
patient with all of them (1 Thess 5:12–14).

Brothers and sisters, do not be weary in doing what is
right. Take note of those who do not obey what we say
in this letter; have nothing to do with them, so that
they may be ashamed. Do not regard them as enemies,
but warn them as believers (2 Thess 3:13–15).

There is no question, therefore, that this work of mercy is
rooted in Scripture and the constant practice of the Church.
All the same, as we noted above, it may seem out of synch
with contemporary trends. Does not this work of mercy presume a judgmental attitude toward others? The trouble with
this spiritual work of mercy is that it seems to contradict contemporary social expectations when it comes to dealing with
people who make choices contrary to traditional morality, for
example. Like it or not, we live in an era of social and moral
relativism, where the only socially acceptable attitude seems
to be, "Everybody has a right to do their own thing, and as
long as no one gets hurt you should never judge anyone else
for their choices or actions."

Thus, for example, if a young—or older—couple chooses
to "live together"—to use the contemporary euphemism for
what earlier, less tolerant, generations called "shacking up" or
"living in sin"—the only socially acceptable response today is
one of polite indifference. In other words, the prejudice has
reversed itself from one of disapproval to tolerance and even
approval. No matter that empirical studies consistently reveal
that couples who cohabit prior to, or instead of, marriage have
a divorce or separation rate double that of couples who do not
cohabit prior to, or instead of, marriage. In other words, the
contemporary attitude amounts to one that says, "Don't con-
fuse us with the facts."

The spiritual work of mercy called "admonish the sinner" reminds us that far from being an act of intolerance and condemnation, to "admonish" a couple who "lives together"—to stay with the example we've been using so far—is an act of mercy. Before we go any further, however, let's take a look at our terms.

The first dictionary definition of "admonish" is "to reprove gently but earnestly."[40] Notice that nowhere in this definition is there any hint of condemnation or personal rejection. In other words, to "admonish" someone for making what clearly is a dangerous, risky, or unhealthy choice—such as "living together"—does not include alienating yourself from him or her. To admonish does not include saying you'll never speak to the person again unless he or she reverses the choice in question. To admonish means you "gently but earnestly" point out the likely consequences of the choice the person is making.

The second key word here is "sinner." This is a term not so easy to understand today. Simplistic notions of sin are possible today only for the simpleminded. A theological dictionary defines "sin" as

> ...any thought, word, or deed that deliberately disobeys God's will and in some way rejects the divine goodness and love.... The Catholic tradition, like Western Christianity generally, has tended to think of the sins of individuals rather than of the community wounded by sin. But the 1987 encyclical of John Paul II, *Sollicitudo rei socialis*...witnesses to a renewed sense of the societal dimension of sin....[41]

In order to better understand "sinner," however, we need to look at yet another word, and that word is "culpable." This is a term used by moral theologians and ethicists. It means "deserving of blame or censure as being wrong, evil, improper, or injurious."[42] The distinction moral theologians make is that a person may sin, but he or she may not be culpable due to the presence of circumstances or conditions which reduce or even eliminate his or her ability to choose freely. Thus, to use an extreme example, a person may kill another person but due to mental illness or serious psychological instability he or she may not be culpable, or blameworthy.

If we apply this insight to a young man and woman who choose to cohabit, or "live in sin," it may be objectively evident that this choice is not a good choice and not a healthy choice for them as individuals and for the long-range health of their relationship. At the same time, we may need to admit that we cannot view this young couple apart from the popular culture in which they have lived their entire lives, a popular culture which has a ho-hum attitude towards "living together" prior to or apart from marriage. Thus, this young couple may not be culpable, or at least their blameworthiness is considerably mitigated by the heavy influence of the popular culture on their attitudes and values with regard to the question of cohabitation.

To return to the societal dimension of sin, mentioned above, this may be an excellent example of how the wider society is far more blameworthy, or culpable, than particular couples who choose to "live together." The social nature of sin seems evident in this example. In this case—as in many others if we stop to think about it—the "sinner" that needs to be "admonished" isn't a particular person but the dominant culture and society at large. The issue of nonmarital cohabitation and its long-range negative impact on marriages or—to use another contemporary euphemism—"relationships" is one that needs to be brought to the attention of society at large, but we rarely hear anything about it—except from evangelical Protestant communities and the occasional conservative Catholic sector.

As far as those outside the "relationship" are concerned—

parents and friends of couples who choose to "live together"—
typically the most they can do by way of "admonishing the
sinner," to quote words from earlier in this chapter, is to "'gently
but earnestly' point out the likely consequences of the choice"
the couple is making. Lecturing, engaging in moralistic ha-
rangues, or threatening to "never speak to you again" is an
approach that will result only in anger, bad feelings, and alienation. Threatening, in effect, to emotionally ostracize the couple
isn't what this work of mercy means by "admonishing."

It can help to remember, again, that persons who make
what appear to be sinful choices in many cases—certainly in
cases where couples choose to "live in sin"—have probably
lived their entire lives in a culture that has no problem with
cohabitation. Unless the young man and woman were fortunate enough to experience effective catechesis during their early
and later adolescent years—not a common phenomenon in the
Catholic Church in the United States since the late 1960s and
even before that—in all likelihood they are as much victims of
the popular culture as anything else. Parents and friends do
well to keep this in mind and place the emphasis on "gentle
but earnest" when it comes to "admonishing."

The same goes for any other form of "sinfulness." If a
friend or loved one is clearly engaged in some "thought, word,
or deed that deliberately disobeys God's will and in some way
rejects the divine goodness and love"—to use the definition of
sin given above—then it would be an act of mercy to "gently
but earnestly" point out to him or her the likely consequences
of this choice or behavior. Why focus on consequences? Because one thing you can count on with regard to sin is that its
consequences are invariably unpleasant to downright painful,
regardless of how pleasant or gratifying this choice or behavior may seem at first.

Of course, once again there are phrases here that require
some scrutiny. "God's will" and "rejects the divine goodness

and love" are often not as easy to identify as we might think. Obvious sins, like murder, stealing, adultery, and dishonesty of various sorts, are not difficult to identify. Even a sin such as fornication—casual sexual intercourse between an unmarried man and woman—is easy to identify regardless of how socially acceptable it may have become. Such sins are clearly contrary to the will of God because they hurt both those who commit these sins as well as having a negative effect on the quality of relationships in families and in society at large. These acts, therefore, constitute "rejections of the divine goodness and love."

In other situations, however, it's not so easy to determine whether an act disobeys God's will and rejects the divine goodness and love. In fact, quite often it's difficult, if not impossible, for an objective observer to know for certain if someone else's actions are sinful or not. Hence, to stick to our main example so far, the riskiness of telling a cohabiting couple that they're "living in sin." Objectively speaking, "living together" is sinful, yes, because it is so likely to be damaging or even destructive to the long-range health of the relationship or eventual marriage. But, as we noted above, we need to keep in mind the cultural conditioning the couple has been subject to for virtually their entire lives.

Most couples who choose to cohabit have no real awareness of the riskiness of their choice to "live together" and be sexually active without being married first. Many such couples are, in fact, utterly clueless, but through virtually no fault of their own. Therefore it makes little sense to accuse them of "living in sin." The time for equipping them to adopt a more critical, objective stance toward the dominant culture is, unfortunately, long past by the time they choose cohabitation.

One of the forms that "admonishing the sinner" takes today is more commonly referred to as "intervention." In cases where individuals are engaged in some behavior which is "sinful" in the sense that it is self-destructive—even though the individual may not be fully culpable—a family intervention, in particular, can be one of the most effective ways to "admonish" him or her. Anytime someone needs help but refuses to accept it, a family intervention is appropriate.

A family intervention can be used for people engaged in any self-destructive behavior, including a person who abuses alcoholic beverages, an anorexic, a gambler, a computer addict, someone in the grip of a sexual addiction (for example, pornography), or an older person who needs to be in an assisted living situation. Intervention can be the most loving, helpful, and effective way to assist someone to get help.

A family intervention can be done with love and respect in a nonconfrontational, nonjudgmental manner. A family intervention is often the answer; in fact, sometimes it is the only answer.

A common scenario might look like this:

*The Preparation:* Family and friends may initially be apprehensive and confused. They may be ambivalent about whether or not to do the intervention. Some may be afraid of the person, others may be angry. The goal is to move from this disorganized and chaotic state to a cohesive, focused group.

To do this, the participants meet with the leader beforehand to educate themselves about the dysfunction, to determine how to best help themselves, and to prepare for Intervention Day. This includes identifying others who should be involved, exploring appropriate treatment options, and preparing what they are going to say. This preparation often involves several meetings, telephone calls, and culminates in a practice session immediately prior to the Intervention Day. The time varies, but the process is usually contained within one to two weeks. Sometimes it can be shortened to a weekend.

*Family Intervention Day:* Imagine family, friends, colleagues, and an intervention leader entering a man's home or office. As the leader ensures an orderly and safe process, the man hears how much he means to everyone there, how his behavior affects them, and what they want their relationship with him to be in the future. Then the man is asked to accept help now; appropriate arrangements are already in place. The tone is loving, respectful, and supportive, but firm; there is no debate. Seeing his many loved ones, friends and colleagues together, the man hears what they say and knows he can no longer hide his problem. Nor does he want to.

In a short time he is receiving help. Following Family Intervention Day much remains to be done. The education process continues. Participants follow through on their plans for helping themselves. It is never business as usual again.

*Family Interventions Vary:* Because each family situation is different, the scope and approach to each intervention must vary accordingly. What may be practical and appropriate for one family may not be for another. For example, some family interventions require several weeks of preparation, others can be done in a few hours or days. Most family interventions have a professional leader present, others not. Often a family intervention occurs in the person's home, others in the leader's office. Some are a surprise, others are not. Sometimes a great deal of family education takes place before the intervention, in others it takes place afterward. Contact the Intervention Center to discuss a family intervention for your situation.[43]

A word of caution is important, here. Family interventions are, invariably, difficult. So it is vitally important that they be carried out as they should be by people who are well prepared. A family intervention should never be planned unless you have the guidance of a professional who is experienced with the intervention process. Virtually always, the professional should be present for the intervention and during other critical times in the process.

Finally, those who decided to carry out an intervention frequently have mixed feelings, and they are often nervous and uncertain. So it is critical that they have complete trust in the professional interventionist. If you ever feel uncomfortable with the professional you're working with, or if you feel that you are being asked to proceed with some action that you don't understand or don't agree with, don't hesitate to bring the process to an end and look for help someplace else.

Another context in which we can look at this spiritual work of mercy is that of marriage. There are both healthy and unhealthy ways in which we can understand the idea of "admonishing the sinner" on the domestic scene.

Anyone who works with engaged and/or married couples will tell you that one of the most dangerous assumptions a spouse can have is that it is his or her job to change the other spouse. There are countless stories of marriages that ended in divorce primarily because either husband or wife decided prior to the wedding that he or she could reform the other spouse once they were married. The underlying presumption is that some behavior of the other spouse is, first of all, "bad," and second of all, that if he or she really loves me he or she will stop this behavior.

One of the classic situations involves a spouse who abuses alcohol or drugs. The other spouse thinks, "After we're married, I'll get him/her to stop drinking" or "After we're married, I'll get him/her to stop abusing drugs." If this spouse is a

Catholic, he or she might even think explicitly in terms of the spiritual work of mercy at hand. "It will be my job as the spouse to 'admonish the sinner' and get this behavior to stop. It's obviously sinful, and it's my job to stop it."

In the first place, alcohol abuse or drug abuse is more likely to be an illness than a moral failure. Consequently, it's inappropriate to think in terms of acting on a spiritual work of mercy here. In the second place, if there is one truth that experts on marriage will insist upon it's that no one can "make" someone else change his or her behavior. It's a pipe dream to think that you can ever change your spouse's behavior to suit your preferences, no matter how objectionable that behavior may be.

"To admonish the sinner" is, in fact, a gentle act of kindness and an expression of unconditional love for another person, not a way to subtly judge or condemn someone else under the cloak of true religion. The only way to "admonish" anyone is with humility and quiet joy. Then, once the "admonishing" is over, you both get on with your lives knowing that you remain on good terms and are both loved unconditionally by God.

CHAPTER 9

# To Instruct the Ignorant

This spiritual work of mercy does not refer merely to a condition of "ignorance" as this term is typically understood. We're not talking about the simple lack of knowledge, as in, "He is ignorant of the rules of baseball." Rather, this spiritual work of mercy refers to "ignorance" in a particularly moral sense. Here, *ignorance* refers to "the absence of information which one is required to have."[44] The emphasis is on the idea that this is not just any information but information that "one is *required* to have." In other words, a person is required, in virtue of his or her humanity, to have and live in the light of this knowledge. One of the most obvious examples of this would be the requirement to know the difference between right and wrong.

Thus, we are required by our humanity to gain not just information we can use for practical purposes. We are required to become well-educated persons in every sense; we are to gain not just "job skills," for example, but we are to gain what we might call "interior formation." Our education, formal and informal, should help us to become people who can act not just from the intellect but from the heart as well.

Thus, "to instruct the ignorant" is to help others gather the kinds of education and moral and spiritual formation that

84

will enable them to function in the world as complete human persons. This is one of the reasons that catechesis and a basic education in the humanities are essential to any complete formation during a person's younger years. Indeed, this is a process that should be lifelong, for no one ever reaches a point where his or her education, in this sense, is complete.

For some people, including parents and teachers, "to instruct the ignorant" is basic to their vocations. Parents and teachers are obliged to provide practical, moral, and spiritual formation for the children and young people they serve. Even Catholic teachers who work in nonchurch related schools are obliged to provide moral and spiritual formation for children, if not by their words—which may be prohibited by government regulations—at the very least by the example of their actions and by answering honestly any questions students may raise about moral and spiritual questions or issues.

But there are ways that this spiritual work of mercy belongs to the vocation of any baptized Christian. We live in a pluralistic culture, one in which many lifestyles, philosophies, and religions must exist side-by-side in mutual respect. This is particularly true of the workplace. A person is as likely as not to work alongside people of a variety of philosophical and religious convictions or no particular philosophical or religious convictions at all. Of course, the dominant culture discourages talking about one's philosophical or religious beliefs in social situations. Anyone who does make others uncomfortable is likely to be dismissed as "some kind of religious nut."

All the same, there are important ways that anyone can "instruct the ignorant" that don't require verbalizing. Indeed, Saint Francis of Assisi once said that one should proclaim the Gospel always, and if necessary sometimes use words. It is our actions that matter most when it comes to providing others with instruction in the Christian life.

Sometimes we overlook ways that this spiritual work of

mercy is carried out because they are right in front of us and we take them for granted. Take, for example, the work of Catholic writers and journalists. By means of the printed word, Catholic writers and journalists help all of us to overcome our ignorance of the meaning of the Gospel for our own time and place. Journalists do their work through newspapers and magazines, often at a significant sacrifice because working for a Catholic newspaper or magazine is hardly a way to join the ranks of the rich. Catholic journalists "instruct the ignorant" by reporting on the news of the day in the light of the Gospel and by writing about people in whose lives the faith of the God's people is alive and active on a day-in, day-out basis.

Catholic writers include those who write both fiction and nonfiction, and it's not unusual for most to write both on various occasions. It's not difficult, of course, to see how writing nonfiction can be a way to "instruct the ignorant" by helping us to gain a better or deeper understanding of our faith and of truths that we need to understand in order to live our faith in more mature ways. Two Catholic writers of our time who do this by writing both nonfiction and fiction are the late André Dubus and Ron Hansen.

André Dubus wrote books of essays about a variety of topics, but they always included at least a few essays on explicitly faith-related topics. Sometimes he helps readers to gain a deeper empathy for those who live their faith while living with physical disabilities, because Dubus himself spent the last several years of his life in a wheelchair following an accident that left him with one leg and an inability to walk. In the title essay in his book *Broken Vessels* André Dubus wrote, for example, about both his physical disability and his two young daughters from his marriage that ended in divorce:

A week ago I read again *The Old Man and the Sea* [by
Ernest Hemingway], and learned from it that, above
all, our bodies exist to perform the condition of our
spirits: our choices, our desires, our loves. My physical
mobility and my little girls have been taken from me;
but I remain. So my crippling is a daily and living sculp-
ture of certain truths: we receive and we lose, and we
must try to achieve gratitude; and with that gratitude
to embrace with whole hearts whatever of life that remains after the losses. No one can do this alone, for
being absolutely alone finally means a life not only
without people or God or both to love, but without
love itself. In *The Old Man and the Sea*, Santiago is a
widower and a man who prays; but the love that fills
and sustains him is of life itself: living creatures, and
the sky, and the sea. Without that love, he would be an
old man alone in a boat.[45]

André Dubus took not only his own experience but the
writing of Ernest Hemingway—hardly a dyed-in-the-wool
Christian writer—and related it all to the meaning of the Gospel. Thus, he "instructs the ignorant' in how to relate faith to
the real world of everyday life. Reading Dubus's words we
can, in turn, attempt to carry out the same exercise he did but
by using our own experience and thoughts. Thus, we find ourselves better able to live a grown-up faith.

Another contemporary Catholic writer of both fiction and
nonfiction is Ron Hansen, author of novels such as *Mariette
in Ecstasy* and *Hitler's Niece*. In both cases, Hansen "instructs
the ignorant." In an essay on faith and fiction, Hansen explains how fiction inspired by faith isn't the same as so-called
"religious fiction," including the hundreds of volumes of "Christian fiction" that issue from evangelical publishers every year
and sell like hot dogs at a boy scout picnic:

A faith-inspired fiction squarely faces the imponderables of life, and in the fiction writer's radical self-confrontation may even confess to desolation and doubt. Such writing is instinctive rather than conformist, intuitive rather than calculated; it features vital characters rather than comforting types, offers freedom and anomaly rather than foregone conclusions, invites thoughtfulness not through rational argument, but through asking the right questions. A faith-inspired fiction is, as Anthony de Mello has said, the shortest distance between human understanding and truth.

While it may be hard to believe now, in the late nineteenth century Cardinal John Henry Newman was forced to defend having literature courses at all in a Catholic university. His argument was "if Literature is to be made a study of human nature, you cannot have a Christian Literature. It is a contradiction in terms to attempt a sinless Literature of sinful man. You may gather together something very great and high, something higher than Literature ever was; and when you have done so, you will find that it is not Literature at all."[46]

Faith-inspired fiction "instructs the ignorant" not by means of pious allegory or thinly cloaked sermonizing, but by telling stories that reflect the ambiguous, complex world that is filled with ambiguous, complex people who have ambiguous, complex relationships. Ron Hansen's novel *Hitler's Niece*, for example, or Graham Greene's modern classic *The Heart of the Matter* can teach the reader more about authentic faith than a truckload of bestsellers based on fundamentalist interpretations of Scripture.[47]

Scobie, the main character in Greene's novel, has committed suicide, and his wife is sure that he went straight to hell.

"It's no good even praying," she laments. The priest, Father Rank, responds impatiently:

> "For goodness' sake, Mrs. Scobie, don't imagine you—
> or I—know a thing about God's mercy."
>     "The Church says..."
>     "I know the Church says. The Church knows all
> the rules. But it doesn't know what goes on in a single
> human heart."
>     "You think there's some hope then?" she wearily
> asked.
>     "Are you so bitter against him?"
>     "I haven't any bitterness left."
>     "And do you think God's likely to be more bitter
> than a woman?" he said with harsh insistence, but she
> winced away from the arguments of hope.
>     "Oh, why, why, did he have to make such a mess
> of things?"
>     Father Rank said, "It may seem an odd thing to
> say—when a man's as wrong as he was—but I think,
> from what I saw of him, that he really loved God."
>     She had denied just now that she felt any bitter-
> ness, but a little more of it drained out now like tears
> from exhausted ducts. "Her certainly loved no one
> else," she said.
>     "And you may be in the right of it there too," Fa-
> ther Rank replied.[48]

Another example from contemporary fiction is the often anthologized short story by André Dubus (d. 1999), "A Father's Story." In this story Luke Ripley is the father of an adult daughter and a devout Catholic. He describes himself as the owner of a stable with thirty horses where his employees give riding lessons. One day while driving her car Luke's daughter accidentally hits and kills a man walking along the side of a rural two-lane road. Luke, desperate to save his daughter from prosecution, covers up for her so she won't be prosecuted for killing the man. Luke knows that what he has done is wrong, and it alters forever the way he experiences his life:

> I do not feel the peace I once did: not with God, nor the earth, or anyone on it. I have begun to prefer this state, to remember with fondness the other one as a period of peace I neither earned nor deserved. Now in the mornings while I watch purple finches driving larger titmice from the feeder, I say to Him: I would do it again. For when she knocked on my door, then called me, she woke what had flowed dormant in my blood since her birth, so that what rose from the bed was not a stable owner or a Catholic or any other Luke Ripley I had lived with for a long time, but the father of a girl. And He says: I am a Father too.[49]

God then says that he did not spare his own Son from suffering as Luke has spared his daughter. Yes, Luke replies, but if God's child had been a daughter then he could not have allowed her to suffer and die as his Son did. Had one of Luke's sons accidentally killed someone he could have allowed human justice to take its course and even looked on proudly as his son bore the consequences of his actions. But not a daughter.

> So, He says, you love her more than you love Me.
> I love her more than I love truth.

> Then you love me in weakness, He says.
> As You love me, I say...[50]

With his story André Dubus "squarely faces the imponderables of life"—to recall Ron Hansen's words—and thus preserves the mystery of faith and the mystery of God's relationship with real, complex human beings. Dubus refuses to write pious stories that are little more than allegories. Instead, he instructs the reader about the truth of human existence and the truth of God's love, not for two-dimensional characters but for real, unpredictable people like you and me.

Finally, one of the best examples of a modern Catholic writer of fiction who wrote about faith without merely churning out pious allegories was Flannery O'Connor. In her posthumous collection of essays on writing, *Mystery and Manners*, O'Connor wrote:

> If I had to say what a "Catholic novel" is, I could only say that it is one that represents reality adequately as we see it manifested in this world of things and human relationships. Only in and by these sense experiences does the fiction writer approach a contemplative knowledge of the mystery they embody.
>
> To be concerned with these things means not only to be concerned with the good in them, but with the evil, and not only with the evil, but also with that aspect which appears neither good nor evil, which is not yet Christianized....This all means that what we roughly call the Catholic novel is not necessarily about a Christianized or Catholicized world, but simply that it is one in which the truth as Christians know it has been used as a light to see the world by.[51]

O'Connor's many short stories, and her novels—most notably *Wise Blood*—frequently feature grotesque, bizarre characters. All the same, these stories, for the alert reader, constitute instruction for the ignorant in the nature and purpose of authentic Christian life and faith in the world as it really is.

Of course, the spiritual work of mercy that beckons us "to

instruct the ignorant" can take many forms, and most of us will never be gifted writers like Ron Hansen, Graham Greene, André Dubus, or Flannery O'Connor. Parents and teachers, of course, are in a position almost daily to "instruct the ignorant" in all kinds of ways. But even in our day-to-day interactions with other people we can share our insights on some of life's most significant issues. Take, for example, the ways we react to as simple an experience as watching a movie.

A group of friends attended a screening of the 2002 M. Night Shyamalan sci-fi film *Signs*, starring Mel Gibson. In this film Gibson's character is apparently an Episcopalian priest because he's called "Father," but he is a widowed father of two children, a boy and a girl. The story line focuses on the Gibson character and his family's encounter with space aliens on their Pennsylvania farm. But parallel to this story is a sub-story about the Gibson character's loss of faith following the accidental death of his wife.

As the story moves along, Shyamalan makes it clear that the former clergyman wants nothing to do with a God who would allow his wife to die. At a tense moment he furiously declares that he will never waste another moment of his life praying. At the climax of the film one of the space aliens enters the farmhouse where the Gibson character, his younger brother—a former minor league star baseball player—and the two children have barricaded themselves in the basement. The boy has asthma, and the adults forgot to bring his medication down into the basement. An attack of asthma leaves the boy unconscious, but by the next morning the space alien has apparently gone, so back up into the house the little group goes— only to discover that the space alien is still there.

To get to the main point here, however, the Gibson character's brother attacks the space alien with a baseball bat, and a glass of water spills on the alien, which has a deadly effect, but not before the alien sprays the little boy with a mysterious gas.

The former clergyman, played by Mel Gibson, dramatically cradles his son in his arms, gives him an injection of his asthma medication, and apparently prays for his son's life to be saved. The boy recovers, and in the movie's final scene Gibson's character is back in his clerical suit, his faith restored. In other words, the character lost his faith—and his vocation—because his wife was killed in an accident. But his faith returned when his son's life was spared by an apparent minor miracle.

Discussing the film, most of those in the group expressed admiration for Mel Gibson's character. One person, however, pointed out that the character's faith was flimsy at best. What kind of faith, she asked, disappears because of the death of a spouse then returns just a quickly because a son escapes death? This was a good example of someone "instructing the ignorant" on what authentic faith is and is not in an informal but real way. It's the kind of "instructing the ignorant" that anyone can do in all kinds of everyday ways.

## CHAPTER 10

# To Counsel the Doubtful

In the context of faith, the idea of doubt can have a spooky sound to it, for some folks at least. There can be a tendency to think of doubt as the opposite of faith, as if to have doubts is to not have faith. Let's look at both of these words, then, and make sure we understand what we're talking about here. We need to do this before we can understand this particular spiritual work of mercy.

In a Catholic faith context, "doubt" actually seems to have three meanings. In canon law, "doubt" refers to "the inability of an individual to make a judgment between two probable opinions. Doubt is not the same thing as error, that is, a mistaken judgment...."[52] In other words, this meaning refers to "a doubt of law."[53]

One example of this kind of doubt would be that between 1983, when the church's Code of Canon Law was revised, and 1994 there was doubt about whether girls could be altar servers. This doubt was resolved in 1994 when the Church's official teaching office ("the Holy See") issued a statement affirming that girls and women could be altar servers. Prior to this, legitimate doubt existed and at such times the Code of Canon Law (can. 14) says that a law need not be obeyed. Thus, it was perfectly acceptable for parishes to have female altar servers prior to the official statement on this question between 1983 and 1994.

The second meaning of "doubt" in a Catholic faith context is the "mental uncertainty regarding the morality of a contemplated action or lack of action."[54] You may have a clear grasp of a particular moral requirement—to not steal, for example—but you may all the same have what's called "practical uncertainty" about living out this law in particular circumstances. A simplistic example would be a situation in which you are hungry but have no money to buy food, and a soup kitchen you know of doesn't open for several hours. Is it okay to steal some food in the mean time? You may have a "mental uncertainty" about this, that is, a doubt.

The third meaning of "doubt" is the one that most people may think of when they think of "doubt" in the context of Catholic faith. This meaning refers to "uncertainty about or suspension of assent to particular Christian beliefs or even to the faith as a whole."[55] Thus, you may be uncertain about the perpetual virginity of Mary, the mother of Jesus. Or you may find yourself unable to agree that the story of Jesus walking on the water in the gospels is literally, historically true. Or again, you may at times find yourself wondering if you can believe even the most basic teachings of Christianity as articulated, for example, in the Apostles' Creed.

Now that we have laid out the three meanings of "doubt" this spiritual work of mercy called "to counsel the doubtful" may not seem as simple as it did in the first place. If we are to counsel the doubtful it's possible that the person's doubts may fall into any of the three categories we discussed above. He or she—or perhaps even a whole parish community—may have doubts about some point of church law regarding liturgical practices, for example. A married couple may be struggling with the morality of family planning methods. Or someone you know may doubt that Jesus could have been literally conceived totally apart from human sexual intercourse. Anyone may find himself or herself in a position to "counsel the doubtful" in any of these or countless other situations where doubt is present. The question becomes, then, what are we supposed to do? Exactly how are we supposed to go about counseling someone who is doubtful?

In situations where the first two kinds of doubt are present—with regard to observance of Church law or the morality of specific actions or choices—if you are reasonably well informed about the issue the person has doubts about, you can probably be helpful simply by offering information. You can say that if doubt about the particular law is more or less widespread in the church then it's probably okay to go ahead and do what the person thinks is best. If the person is uncertain about the morality of a particular choice or action you can advise him or her to seek more information and guidance from persons who are better informed or from books that discuss the choice or action under consideration.

If a person has doubts about particular Christian or specifically Catholic beliefs or doctrines, it's important first of all to be a good listener. It's not unusual for people with doubts of this sort to have more going on "beneath the surface," spiritually and/or psychologically and emotionally, than just—as counselors say—"the presenting issue." A person may express doubts about anything from the divinity and humanity of Christ to the infallibility of the pope; from the virginal conception of Jesus to the official Church theological position that women cannot be ordained as priests. Someone may say that he or she can't believe that Jesus fed thousands of people with two loaves of bread and a few fish, or that he brought Lazarus back to life after he had been dead for three days. Or, a person may express doubts about the truth of the Christian religion, lock, stock, and barrel.

In each of these examples, the person may well have actual

mental reservations or doubts that keep him or her from accepting the truth of the particular belief, teaching, or doctrine—or of the Christian religion as a whole. If this is the case, the most important response is to listen without condemning or even judging. Sometimes, especially if you're a parent listening to the doubts expressed by an adolescent or young adult offspring, the temptation can be to express shock then go on a rant of one kind or another. Not a good idea. When this chapter's spiritual work of mercy advises counseling the doubtful it doesn't mean you should faint dead away or threaten eternal punishment for "having doubts."

We need to keep in mind that, in fact, if a person has never had any doubts about his or her faith it's probably not much of a faith.[56] Faith is faith, and one of the best ways to understand faith is to compare it to a relationship between two people, especially a marriage or close friendship. Before it is anything else, faith is a relationship between God and us, both as a community and each one of us as individuals. Specifically Christian faith is loving intimacy between the risen Christ and his people, the Church. It is because we belong to and participate in the life of the community we call "Church" that we "have faith" as individuals.

The reason doubt is, in fact, inseparable from faith is because this relationship we call faith is between the infinite God and we finite humans, and it's impossible for a finite human to fully comprehend the infinite God. Therefore, faith is bound to include uncertainty. The truth is that it is more accurate to say that by faith we are comprehended by God than vice versa. Faith involves trust the way a loving marriage or close friendship involves trust. Husband and wife trust each other, and two friends trust each other, without fully understanding each other. Rather, we accept the mystery of the other and place our trust in him or her, without demanding that we have full understanding as a prerequisite to trust. The same is true of faith.

We give ourselves to Christ, and through him to the One we are instructed to call Father, out of love and without demanding that we fully grasp the mystery of this faith beforehand.

Perhaps the best-known description of faith occurs in the so-called "Letter" to the Hebrews: "Now faith is the assurance of things hoped for, the conviction of things not seen" (11:1). Note, this is a partial *description* of faith, not a *definition*. These words tell us something important about what faith *does*. Faith gives us "assurance of things hoped for" and makes it possible for us to be convinced about the reality of "things not seen." This is another reason that faith is bound to include doubts, because the "things" this description refers to remain "hoped for" and "not seen."

If someone, anyone, expresses faith-related doubts, this is simply an admission that he or she is human. "Counseling the doubtful" comes into the picture, first, when we *listen* sympathetically. At the same time, it can be helpful to both share our own doubts—and it's important that we not pretend that we have no doubts about anything faith-related—and at the same time share our experiences of God's love in our own life. We can share about the ways that, in spite of our doubts, we remain convinced about the reality of "things not seen."

It is a mistake for any Catholic to presume that genuine faith has no questions or doubts about anything. Rather, the only kind of "faith" that has no questions or doubts is the kind of "faith" we find in people who belong to cults of various sorts. Surprising as it may be, sometimes even well-established religious institutions can be cults—the Mormon Church, for example. The Church of Jesus Christ of Latter Day Saints (LDS) specializes in doing whatever is necessary to spare its members from having doubts about their faith. As journalist-historian Richard Abanes explains, considerable academic dishonesty goes on among Mormons to make sure that any Mormon history they learn about is "faith-promoting":

In other words, books read by Mormons are intention-
ally designed to build up their faith, not challenge it in
any way, especially on an intellectual basis. Since its
earliest days, Mormonism has been an emotion-based
religion opposed to intellectual, rational thought. Po-
tential converts were told in the 1800s, just as they are
instructed now, to "feel" the validity of Mormonism
independent of reasoning.

This "feeling," often described as a "burning in
the bosom," allegedly is the "witness of the Spirit" (that
is, God) that Mormonism is true. Although the "feeling" is completely subjective, its power over Mormons
cannot be overstated. Even when faced with irrefut-
able facts that undermine the LDS church, a Saint [that
is, member of the Mormon church] will cling to their
"witness" and often resort to simply repeating their personal testimony, as a kind of mantra that helps them
sustain a state of unthinking, faith-bolstering denial.
They will say something like: "I bear you my testimony
that Joseph Smith [that is, the mid-nineteenth-century
founder of Mormon church] was a prophet of God,
that the Church of Jesus Christ of Latter-day Saints is
the only true church, and that the *Book of Mormon* is
true."

Such a response also shows obedience to LDS lead-
ers, who have counseled their followers to not only
shun anything that might shake their faith, but also to
simply not think and obey church authorities.[57]

The Catholic view of faith and doubt is directly opposed
to anything like this. Some very conservative Catholics may,
unfortunately, give the impression that a Catholic's obedience
to the pope, and official Church teachings, must amount to blind
faith, but this simply is not true. The only ultimate authority

for Catholicism is the well-formed conscience of the individual, *even if that conscience is in error*. Sometimes conservative Catholics seem to say that there can never be any difference between a well-formed conscience and an official teaching of the Church. As the *Catechism of the Catholic Church* explains, however:

> A human being must always obey the certain judgment of his conscience. If he were deliberately to act against it, he would condemn himself.[58]

For Catholicism, faith is never about not thinking. The idea of "blind faith," a faith that refuses to use the brains God gave us, is a perversion of authentic faith. True faith has doubts, and asks questions, and involves the intellect. Some of the most familiar lines in the New Testament reflect the fact that from very early in the history of Christianity this was believed to be so. Consider the lines from the Gospel of Luke that tell of the absolutely critical moment in the history of salvation, the encounter between Mary and the angel Gabriel:

> In the sixth month the angel Gabriel was sent by God to a town in Galilee called Nazareth, to a virgin engaged to a man whose name was Joseph, of the house of David. The virgin's name was Mary. And he came to her and said, "Greetings, favored one! The Lord is with you." But she was much perplexed by his words and pondered what sort of greeting this might be. The angel said to her, "Do not be afraid, Mary, for you have found favor with God. And now, you will conceive in your womb and bear a son, and you will name him Jesus. He will be great, and will be called the Son of the Most High, and the Lord God will give to him the throne of his ancestor David.

He will reign over the house of Jacob forever, and of his kingdom there will be no end." Mary said to the angel, "How can this be, since I am a virgin?"

The angel said to her, "The Holy Spirit will come upon you, and the power of the Most High will over-shadow you; therefore the child to be born will be holy; he will be called Son of God (1:26–35).

Notice, Mary shows no sign of a "blind faith." She has her doubts about this whole business. Luke tells us that she is "perplexed," and then he says that she "pondered," which a dictionary defines as "to reflect in the mind with thoroughness and care." After the angel explains to Mary what's going on, and reassures her, she still isn't satisfied. She questions the angel, asking "How can this be since I am a virgin?" Young Mary knows the score, and she is not about to be taken in by anyone, not even an angel. She has her doubts, and she has her questions, and she is not about to go along with anything that makes no sense to her.

If the Gospel of Luke has no qualms about a portrayal of Mary as a model of discipleship, and a model of faith, that clearly includes doubts and questions, there should be little doubt that for us faith not only can, but should, include doubts and questions. At the same time, sometimes we can be uncomfortable about this. We may doubt that doubt is okay. So those who "counsel the doubtful" may find themselves in the interesting position of needing to *encourage* and *support* doubting and questioning.

Let's return, however, to the third definition of "doubt" explained above, namely, "uncertainty about or suspension of assent to particular Christian beliefs or even to the faith as a whole." We'll take the first part first. If you find yourself called upon by circumstances to counsel someone who is doubtful about a "particular Christian belief," it is important to realize that not all Christian beliefs are equal. Some are essential, some are not, and even among the essential ones there is a hierarchy of importance. Perhaps the example easiest to understand is the New Testament. There are some New Testament documents that are more important, and carry more weight, than others. The four gospels are more important than, say, the Letter of Jude. The Letter of Paul to the Romans is more important than the Second Letter of Peter. And so forth.

Just so, the Christian belief in the Incarnation—"that for the salvation of the world, the Son of God, while remaining fully divine, became truly and fully human…"[59]—is more important than, say, belief in infant baptism. This means, therefore, that to doubt the Incarnation is a more serious matter than to doubt the practice of infant baptism. Even when someone has doubts about a more-or-less central Christian belief, however—for example, the virginal conception of Jesus—this is no cause for a major crisis of faith on the part of the doubter. Even if the person decides that there is no way he or she can accept this belief, this is still no reason to abandon the Catholic faith entirely, or announce that he or she will never participate in the Mass again.

To "counsel" someone who has doubts of this sort, or questions, it is important to encourage the person to simply live with the doubts and questions. It is good to advise the person to take these doubts and questions to God in prayer, and even to offer them to God asking for the grace to deal with them. Doubts about virtually anything related to faith are never a cause for hopelessness or despair.

Finally, however, we need to respond to some words of Jesus in the gospels that seem to say that doubt and faith are incompatible:

> "Truly I tell you, if you say to this mountain, 'Be taken
> up and thrown into the sea,' and if you do not doubt in

your heart, but believe that what you say will come to pass, it will be done for you" (Mk 11:23).

Jesus answered them, "Truly I tell you, if you have faith and do not doubt, not only will you do what has been done to the fig tree, but even if you say to this mountain, 'Be lifted up and thrown into the sea,' it will be done" (Mt 21:21).

Jesus immediately reached out his hand and caught him, saying to him, "You of little faith, why did you doubt?" (Mt 14:31)

Then he said to Thomas, "Put your finger here and see my hands. Reach out your hand and put it in my side. Do not doubt but believe" (Jn 20:27).

In each of these sayings Jesus puts doubt and faith in opposition, but in each case faith is clearly the most basic kind of faith, namely, *a trusting in one's relationship with him*. None of these examples say anything about having questions about specific beliefs, or doctrines, or religious traditions, or practices. In each case, Jesus encourages the kind of faith—complete trust in him—that is deeper than any doubt or question about a particular *expression* of faith or a particular teaching *about* faith. The kind of faith Jesus encourages in each of these instances from the gospels is the kind of faith that is deeper than any doubt or question about specifics. It's the kind of faith that can live with doubts and questions because this faith *is* our intimacy with Christ, running deeper than any doubt.

When we are called upon by circumstances to "counsel the doubtful" it is this deeper, trusting faith that we can remind them about. It is this deeper, trusting faith that we can remind them about, this deeper trusting faith that they may not realize is still there, no matter what.

## CHAPTER II

# To Comfort the Sorrowful

S orrow" is one of those words that can seem so… well, so
*big*, so *overwhelming*, so… *unmanageable*. The causes of
human sorrow seem so *endless*. There are some wonderful
Catholic devotional prayers that seem to both sum up all the
sources of human sorrow and at the same time provide responses to all the sorrows that afflict people. Taken together,
these prayers may seem rather long, but stick with it:

*Let thy mercy, O Lord, be upon us according as we
hope in thee. Our Lady of Sorrows, we pray for those
who will die today because of war, economic chaos,
injustice, and exploitation, especially the children. Prepare them for the agony, despair, and terror of the violence that is upon them. Comfort them and hold them
close to the bosom of thy Wounded Heart as they drink
deeply of the bitter cup which is forced upon them.
Wipe their tears, calm their fears, welcome them to
peace and safety. Eternal rest grant to them, and may
perpetual light shine upon them. Holy Mary, Mother
of God, help the helpless, strengthen the fearful, comfort the sorrowful, bring justice to the poor, peace to all
nations, and solidarity among all peoples. Overturn*

*the thrones of tyranny and scatter the unjust. Cast down the bloody rulers who make the cry of the widow and orphan rise to heaven. Open our eyes to see the beauty, joy, redemption, and goodness which comes through obedience to the Gospel of your Son our Lord. Teach us to be a refuge of hope for all who are oppressed by injustice and violence. Give us strength to stand against the demonic powers which prowl about the world seeking the ruin of souls. Amen.*

*O Christ God, Lord of Glory, who gave us joy and blessing from your Mother's womb, have mercy on us and save us. Remember, Saint Joseph, most humble and loving protector of the poor, that no one ever had recourse to your protection or asked your aid without obtaining relief. Confiding therefore in your goodness, we come before you and pray to you on behalf of all those at risk today of war, economic catastrophe, and injustice....Holy Joseph, help the helpless, comfort the dying, bring justice to the poor, and peace to all nations. Bless our enemies with reconciliation, and bless our nation by removing from us the temptations of empire, wealth, violence, and greed, so that we might realize the promise of our ancestors and be a blessing to all the peoples of this good earth.*

*O Christ God, Lord of Glory, who gave us joy and blessing from your Mother's womb, have mercy on us and save us. Saint Michael the Archangel, defend us in battle. Be our shield against the wickedness and snares of the devil. May God rebuke him, we humbly pray, and do thou, O Prince of the Heavenly Host, by the power of God thrust into hell Satan and all the evil spirits which prowl about the world seeking the ruin of souls. O Christ God, Lord of Glory, who gave us*

*joy and blessing from your Mother's womb, have mercy
on us and save us. O Mary, bright dawn of the new
world, Mother of the living, to you do we entrust the
cause of life: Look down, O Mother, upon the vast
numbers of babies not allowed to be born, of the poor
whose lives are made difficult, of men and women who
are victims of brutal violence, of the elderly and the
sick killed by indifference or out of misguided mercy.
Grant that all who believe in your Son may proclaim
the Gospel of life with honesty and love to the people
of our time. Obtain for them the grace to accept that
Gospel as a gift ever new, the joy of celebrating it with
gratitude throughout their lives and the courage to bear
witness to it resolutely, in order to build, together with
all people of good will, the civilization of truth and
love, to the praise and glory of God, the Creator and
lover of life. Amen.*

*O Christ God, Lord of Glory, who gave us joy and
blessing from your Mother's womb, have mercy on us
and save us.*[60]

Prayers such as these seem especially appropriate in a time
when sorrow seems to characterize the lives of so many people
in so many parts of the world. Indeed, sometimes it can seem
that prayer is the only recourse we have in times of sorrow.
Whether that sorrow is close to home or on other continents,
we feel naturally inclined toward prayer as a response.

A dictionary defines sorrow as "mental suffering or pain
caused by injury, loss, or despair." This definition may not go
far enough, however. The truth is that sorrow can easily be
more than mental in nature. Rather, sorrow can easily be a
spiritual experience, one that touches us to the very roots of
our being. Thus, when the spiritual works of mercy advise us

to "comfort the sorrowful" this is more than an obvious suggestion that we be there for those who are obviously sorrowing, to offer them support and encouragement. Rather than being an occasional gesture, "to comfort the sorrowful" is more like a general outlook on life.

For truth to tell, sorrow is a constant characteristic of life from one day to the next. Who does not have virtually constant sorrows, small or large, that they carry in their heart? Indeed, it is not without cause that Catholic devotional prayers sometimes refer to life in this world as a "vale [valley] of tears." If we find that life is characterized by joy, the flip side is that life is also often characterized by sorrow. Therefore, there are always plenty of opportunities to "comfort the sorrowful" as a part of a Christian approach to everyday life.

Much of the time, of course, we keep our sorrows to ourselves. Many parents of adolescent and/or adult offspring, for example, live with sorrow because of choices their almost-grown and/or grown kids have made. It is the rare parent whose grown children have never disappointed their parents or have never failed to live up to parental expectations. Consequently, most parents carry sorrows small and large in their heart—sorrows they keep to themselves, for the most part.

Of course, our sorrows have countless origins. Traditional Catholic devotional spirituality often refers to a source of sorrow as a "cross." We each have our "crosses" to bear, a general reference to Jesus' words in Luke 14:27 and its parallels in the other gospels: "Whoever does not carry the cross and follow me cannot be my disciple." This may not be a strictly accurate theological interpretation of Jesus' words, since the reference is more to Christian discipleship than to simply bearing with life's difficulties. Still, the application of Jesus' words to life's sorrows is legitimate, too. Life is sometimes a "vale of tears," and every life brings with it "crosses," and living a Christian life includes a response to this dark side of life, too.

Knowing all this, learning to "comfort the sorrowful" is basic to a Christian spirituality for everyday life. Knowing that everyone we know and meet, everyone we live and work with, lives with sorrows about which we may never know the particulars should help us to cultivate a daily capacity for compassion and empathy. No matter how troublefree someone's life may seem, everyone has sorrows they may rarely talk about.

An excellent example of what I'm talking about occurs in the classic nineteenth-century novel by George Eliot (Mary Ann Evans), *Silas Marner: The Weaver of Raveloe*.[61] In this story, a man who is a linen weaver, Silas Marner, "worked at his vocation in a stone cottage that stood among the nutty hedgerows near the village of Raveloe." There he is known as a crotchety recluse, and the local children are terrified of him. As it turns out, years before Silas Marner was the victim of a false charge that ended his previously contented life and broke off his engagement with the young woman he loved.

Silas Marner moved to Raveloe where he returned to his work as a linen weaver, thus supporting himself, but from then on he turned in on himself, his sorrow turning his heart to stone. Now his sole focus became to save the coins he earned as a weaver, turning to his growing wealth as the only thing in which he could place his trust and, indeed, the only thing he could love:

> He handled [the coins], he counted them, till their form and colour were like the satisfaction of a thirst to him; but it was only in the night, when his work was done, that he drew them out to enjoy their companionship. He had taken up some bricks in his floor underneath his loom, and here he had made a hole in which he set the iron pot that contained his guineas and silver coins, covering the bricks with sand whenever he replaced them.... But at night came his revelry: at night he closed his

shutters, and made fast his doors, and drew forth is gold. Long ago the heap of coins had become too large for the iron pot to hold them, and he had made for them two thick leather bags, which wasted no room in their resting place, but lent themselves flexibly to every corner. How the guineas shone as they came pouring out of the dark leather mouths!...

He loved the guineas best, but he could not change the silver—the crowns and half-crowns that were his own earnings, begotten by his labour; he loved them all. He spread them out in heaps and bathed his hands in them; then he counted them and set them up in regular piles, and felt their rounded outline between his thumb and fingers, and thought fondly of the guineas...."[62]

The people of Raveloe do not know that Silas Marner is the kind of man he is because of the great sorrow that he conceals in his heart. Of course, Silas Marner is a fictional example of a rather extreme case, but the principle that his story illustrates is just as valid in the lives of countless real people, ourselves included. That is, our present behavior, and the kind of people we are today, comes in no small part from the sorrows we have experienced, as well as the joys. Of course, most often people do not turn in on themselves like Silas Marner. But they may become more guarded, less willing to reveal themselves to others.

From the perspective of the spiritual work of mercy we're reflecting on here, however, if we are to "comfort the sorrowful" we need to be aware that virtually everyone is "sorrowful," probably in more ways than one. This is easy to see in people who are obviously unhappy or whose sorrows are more or less common knowledge. But we need to remember that even people whose lives appear to be "charmed," people who seem to have a perfect marriages, "perfect" children, and no economic anxieties, even they have their sorrows. Just below the surface you may be sure that they have worries about loved ones, sorrowful experiences from the past, and various emotional insecurities.

What this all boils down to is that we are called to integrate into our daily lives an attitude toward others that takes for granted that everyone, but everyone, needs to be comforted in their sorrows, whether they speak of these sorrows or not. The little ways other people irritate us can often be traced to their sorrows. The attitudes they have regarding all kinds of issues and ideas often come from the ways they are dealing with their sorrows. Hence, we can comfort them by simply being patient, tolerant, and understanding.

Here is an example. Frequently, we attribute a person's conservative or liberal ideas and attitudes to his or her intellect. She is a very conservative Catholic, or he is a very liberal Catholic because of *ideas* they have, or *principles* they have adopted. We think religious conservatism or liberalism is merely a way of *thinking* that the person has chosen to adopt. On the contrary, more often than not being conservative or liberal, particularly in a religious sense, comes as a result of *emotional* issues the person is dealing with.

A person who is emotionally insecure, for whatever reasons, is likely to opt for a conservative religious perspective that offers all the answers, and in which religious authority plays a constant role. A person who has trouble dealing with authority, for whatever reasons, is likely to embrace a religious liberalism that wants little input from religious rules and regulations, as well as from religious authorities.

In both cases, the person's choice to practice a very conservative or a very liberal religion may be due to experiences early in life that could easily be called "sorrows." Hence, it makes little sense to argue with the person as if he or she can be talked into a more balanced religious outlook by sheer power of argument and reason. Reason isn't the point, emotional needs are the point, and no one can argue someone out of his or her emotional needs. Rather, in such cases "to comfort the sorrowful" means accepting the person as he or she is and respecting his or her ways of being religious because they are this person's way of dealing with real emotional needs, that is, his or her "sorrows."

Sometimes we can gain new insights if we approach a subject from a new and unusual perspective. Let's see if we can better understand what it means to "comfort the sorrowful" by reflecting on the lyrics of an "old timey" song as featured in the Cohen brothers 2001 film *O Brother, Where Art Thou?* The song is "Man of Constant Sorrow."

> (In constant sorrow through his days.) I am a man of constant sorrow / I've seen trouble all my day. I bid farewell to old Kentucky / The place where I was born and raised. (The place where he was born and raised.) For six long years / I've been in trouble / No pleasures here on earth I found / For in this world I'm bound to ramble I have no friends to help me now. (He has no friends to help him now.) [chorus]

> It's fare thee well my old lover I never expect to see you again / For I'm bound to ride that northern railroad / Perhaps I'll die upon this train. (Perhaps he'll die upon this train.) [chorus]

> You can bury me in some deep valley / For many years where I may lay / Then you may learn to love another While I am sleeping in my grave. (While he is sleeping in his grave.) [chorus] Maybe your friends think / I'm just a stranger My face you'll never see no more. But there is one promise that is given / I'll meet you on God's golden shore. (He'll meet you on God's golden shore.) [chorus] [63]

Remarkable as it may seem, this old song touches on several of the essential themes we need to reflect upon if we want to understand the human experience of sorrow, especially from a Christian perspective.

In the first verse, the singer expresses the common human experience that life always includes more than enough troubles and heartache; so true is that he describes himself as "a man of constant sorrow." Who, at various times in their lives, cannot identify with this? Are there not times when it seems that sorrow is never going to leave us alone? Basic to the singer's continual experience of sorrow is the fact that he has had to leave behind his home "the place where I was born and raised." This is an expression of alienation, a condition of wandering homeless on the earth, a source of sorrow that never goes away.

In verse two, we learn that for "six long years" the singer has known his sorrowful condition, a life devoid of pleasure. Then he restates in other words his expression of homelessness on the earth and adds to this the further sorrow that he is completely without friends. So his alienation is not only existential but social as well.

In the third verse the singer addresses his "old lover" whom he never expects to see again, bidding her good-bye. Why? Because not only is he homeless and friendless, but he is about to become a passenger on a train—in a boxcar, no doubt—which only emphasizes his nomadic, rootless, sorrowful condition. So permanent is this condition that the singer wouldn't be surprised if he were to die while riding the rails. Thus, even his death would occur while he is on the move, completely unsettled and without friends upon the earth.

Verse four continues the singer's words to his unidentified "old lover." He instructs her to put his grave "in some deep valley," a valley being a place of emptiness and solitude. Thus, even in death he expects to be alone, a "man of constant sorrow."

Finally, in the last verse the singer acknowledges that even the friends of his "old lover" are not his friends, for they seem to think of him as nothing but "a stranger." Regardless, she will never see him again. Yet in spite of his sorrowful condition on the earth, constantly alone, on the move, and friendless, he is not without hope. For he believes in "one promise that is given," namely that he will meet her again "on God's golden shore."

"Man of Constant Sorrow" is a complete description of anyone's experience of life's sorrows, sorrows that come from being alone, from having no home, from having no friends, and from being alienated even from those who loved us in the past. In a few compact verses we have a description of what anyone's sorrows add up to, and we can begin to appreciate why others need us to "comfort" them, even if that comforting means simply accepting and welcoming others into our day.

CHAPTER 12

# To Bear Wrongs Patiently

F irst off, let's be clear from the start that this is one spiritual
work of mercy that can be easily misunderstood. The idea
behind "bearing wrongs patiently" is *not* to become a full-
time doormat for other people to walk on. Neither is the idea
here to make a lifestyle out of tolerating social and economic
injustices.

Rather, those who "bear wrongs patiently" are not unaware of the injustice being perpetrated on themselves or others. At the same time, however, they refuse to let the wrong
crush them or deprive them of hope and their belief in good.
To truly bear wrongs patiently requires confidence in oneself
as loved unconditionally by God and a firm trust that in the
long run justice will be done. Also, this spiritual work of mercy
requires trust that trying to love the wrongdoer(s) will eventually and inevitably defeat injustice.

A frequently overlooked source of insight into this spiritual work of mercy is the early fifteenth-century spiritual classic by Thomas à Kempis, *The Imitation of Christ*. Here is one
relevant passage, and the voice speaking is that of Christ:

> Turn over in your mind the heavy trials of others, and
> your own insignificant ones will be easier to bear. If

you do not think they are insignificant, take care that it is not your lack of patience that causes that as well. But whether they are great or small, aim at bearing them all with patience. If you make up your mind to submit to these things patiently, you will be acting wisely and will acquire more merit. Besides, you will find them easier to bear, if you work hard to develop the right attitude and make it into a habit.

You must not say, "I am quite unable to submit to this sort of thing, coming from a man like that; and it is not the sort of thing I should be asked to accept—he has done me a great deal of harm, and accused me of something that never entered my head. Still, I would accept it from another man, provided I thought it the sort of thing I should be asked to accept."

This kind of thinking is very foolish. It is always weighing up what injuries it has received from which people, instead of keeping it in mind that there is a virtue in patience, and that a reward awaits it from God."[64]

Of course, this whole line of thought, and the spiritual work of mercy that comes from it, finds its ultimate source in the New Testament and the example of Jesus who prayed in the Garden of Gethsemane to be delivered but who did not resist when delivered up to execution unjustly. In words from the First Letter of Peter:

For to this you have been called, because Christ also suffered for you, leaving you an example, so that you should follow in his steps. "He committed no sin, and no deceit was found in his mouth" [see Isaiah 53:7]. When he was abused, he did not return abuse; when he suffered, he did not threaten; but he entrusted himself to the one who judges justly (2:21–23).

It's fairly easy to understand this in the context of, say, resistance to social injustices. Such situations tend to be rather dramatic, and they call for plenty of conscious focus. In modern times the best-known examples of this kind of dramatic situation took the form of the nonviolent resistance to social injustice pioneered by Mahatma Gandhi in India and later applied by Martin Luther King, Jr., in the United States. In both cases "to bear wrongs patiently" took the form of high profile nonviolent resistance as a way to bring about social change.

It's the everyday situations, however, when we don't expect to be treated unfairly, when bearing wrongs patiently becomes a real, everyday challenge. Bearing wrongs patiently from the people we live and work with is more likely than involvement in some dramatic instance of social or economic injustice. The "wrongs" we are most commonly called upon to "bear patiently" are the little personal offenses, the rude comments, the times when we are overlooked, taken for granted, or taken advantage of. These moments may come as the result of thoughtlessness on the part of others. They may come because someone is being consciously unkind or even cruel. But they come to everyone, and the idea here is that we can practice a spiritual work of mercy toward the person who is the source of our being treated badly.

It is an act of mercy to not return the biting remark. It is an act of mercy to keep the ol' mouth shut when instead you could toss back an equally biting remark. When you get the dirty end of the stick, it's a work of mercy to not complain or whine about it. When you feel taken for granted it's a work of mercy to not nurture feelings of resentment toward the person who is rude, discourteous, or insensitive.

Before we go any further, however, we need to dispose of any tendency to apply this spiritual work of mercy to situations where actual abuse takes place in domestic situations.

There is absolutely no way in which "to bear wrongs patiently" can or should be applied when, for example, a woman is being battered by her husband—or vice versa, for that matter.[65] Spousal abuse may be defined as "the deliberate attempt by a partner in an intimate relationship to control or intimidate the other partner."[66] Such abuse can be physical, psychological, sexual, or financial.

In such situations, there is no way that the abused person should think in terms of "bearing wrongs patiently" as a virtuous act. Unfortunately, in many cases of spousal abuse the abused person tends to be far too "forgiving" and "patient," far too willing to give the abusing partner "another chance" and/or make excuses for him or her, as if this is "the Christian thing to do." On the contrary, in such situations there is no possible way that the abused partner should allow the abuse to continue in the name of religion.

Sometimes women, particularly, tolerate abuse because they don't want to deprive their children of a two-parent family. In fact, studies show that there is no validity to such a perspective.

Children who witness violence may

- feel frightened confused and unhappy
- behave aggressively
- feel responsible for the violence
- become depressed or even suicidal
- exhibit self destructive, accident-prone behavior
- seek punishment (identified as love) for behavior such as lying or stealing
- adopt rigid gender role identification
- have night time difficulties or physical complaints[67]

Clearly, then, there is no justification for remaining in an abusive relationship "for the sake of the children." There is no way that the abused partner can justify thinking in terms of "bearing wrongs patiently," for children who witness such violence experience negative consequences—exactly the opposite of the hoped-for outcome.

The spiritual work of mercy we're reflecting upon here has nothing to do with tolerating abusive behavior from anyone, in any situation. It isn't about putting up with abuse. Rather, it's about choosing to be patient with rude, insensitive, and impatient people. In extreme circumstances it's about allowing oneself to be on the receiving end of unfair treatment in order to bring about fair treatment for others or to overcome social or economic injustices.

Let's look at two of the more common situations in today's world where "to bear wrongs patiently" is, indeed, a form of spiritual discipline that can be a part of everyday life. The two situations are driving and marriage.

## Driving

No doubt what we refer to as "road rage" existed for a long time before this term came into the common parlance. But the fact that we now have this term suggests that the phenomenon it refers to is a more frequent occurrence than it once was. We hear accounts of drivers on Los Angeles freeways actually pulling out handguns and shooting at each other. Every week there are news accounts of angered drivers yelling and screaming at each other, even sometimes coming to fisticuffs. Drivers whose cars' electric turn signals don't work may rarely use the standard hand signals, but the "obscene gesture" has become an unofficial hand traffic signal that is popular, indeed. There are even cases where people impatient to get out of the church parking lot on Sunday morning have used this particular hand signal, not to mention hurling verbal abuse—all between people who moments before shared a sign of peace and holy Communion. Boggles the mind, does it not?

Much of the conflict between drivers could be short-circuited if more drivers made the effort "to bear wrongs patiently." Say you and another driver both aim for the same parking space, and the other driver whips into the space when he or she clearly knew you intended to park there. You can respond in an indignant fashion or you can bear this little wrong patiently.

Another driver fails to signal for a turn, and consequently you nearly rear-end him or her. You can either lean on your horn and shake your fist at the other driver, or you can take a deep breath and be grateful that the rear-ender didn't happen.

The ways that drivers can "bear wrongs patiently" are virtually endless. But the benefits to society of doing this are virtually endless, too. When you stop to think about it, what good, really, is accomplished by angry ranting and raving at other drivers who drive in a rude or even potentially dangerous fashion? If you're lucky, your angry gesture will merely result in you blowing off steam. If you're not lucky, it will make the other driver angry in return. Then if you're lucky that will be the end of it. But if you're not lucky, the other driver may decide to find a way to "get even" with you, and then the sky's the limit as to where this will go. This is where the fights and the handguns happen....Far better, as a driver, to work on learning "to bear wrongs patiently."

# Marriage

In any interaction between two or more people, of course, there are endless opportunities to "bear wrongs patiently." With no intention whatsoever of doing so, we get on one another's nerves. Our little habits and idiosyncracies are irritating to other people. But marriage is a particularly intense form of relationship. In marriage, the old adage that "familiarity breeds contempt" has endless opportunities to take root and grow. Indeed, we tend to perceive "wrongs" where others would not, so that we find ourselves called upon by this spiritual work of mercy to "bear patiently" words and actions from our spouse that may or may not actually be "wrongs." A particular word or action may be a "wrong" or it may simply be a little something that irritates the daylights out of us. Either way, of course, the right thing to do may be to "bear" it.

Much of the time in marriage, the only right thing to do is "bear" it, regardless of whether it's truly a "wrong" or not. In an era that—rightly so—places a great deal of emphasis on the need for effective communication and conflict resolution skills in marriage, however, there can be a tendency to think that any time I perceive that I am on the receiving end of a "wrong," I need to bring it up for discussion. Sometimes, of course, this is exactly what needs to happen. If I find myself constantly feeling hurt or offended by something my spouse says or does, we need to talk about it. This does not mean, however, that each and every time my spouse says or does something that hurts, offends, or irritates me I need to immediately call for an in-depth communication session.

Naturally, in marriage a man and woman live in close proximity day after day, week after week, month after month, year after year—and there is no way either one can escape being "wronged" by the other. Sometimes this means husband and wife need to talk it out. They need to use their conflict resolution skills and work through their feelings so whatever is coming between them can be neutralized. At the same time, it is also true that there are endless opportunities in marriage to "bear wrongs patiently." There are countless times every day when the right thing to do is tolerate the unfair way my spouse is treating me. Yes, I took out the trash twice this week already, but the fact that my spouse is ignoring the need to take it out again does not mean that I should make a sarcastic remark about it in order to avoid taking out the trash yet again.

On the other hand, maybe I'm the one who has not been taking out the trash this week, and maybe I have simply been oblivious to the trash. Maybe my spouse *does* make a sarcastic remark because it seems to my spouse that it's my turn to take out the trash. Maybe this sarcastic remark takes me completely by surprise. I can either respond sarcastically myself or I can ignore the sarcasm and quietly take out the trash. By "bearing" this wrong "patiently" I neutralize a situation that could easily become very unpleasant for both of us.

Lest we think, however, that this business of bearing wrongs patiently is the purview of the relatively virtuous who must put up with "wrongs" that come from the relatively nonvirtuous, we might consider a poem by the Pulitzer Prize-winning American Catholic poet Phyllis McGinley (1905–1978). In her poem "The Giveaway," McGinley described how stressful it can be to live with an actual saint, in this case the Irish saint, Bridget (c. 450–525):

Saint Bridget was
A problem child.
Although a lass
Demure and mild,
And one who strove
To please her dad,
Saint Bridget drove
The family mad.
For here's the fault in Bridget lay:
She *would* give everything away.

To any soul
Whose luck was out
She'd give her bowl
Of stirabout;
She'd give her shawl,
Divide her purse
With one and all.

And what was worse,
When she ran out of things to give
She'd borrow from a relative.

Her father's gold,
Her grandsire's dinner,
She'd hand to cold
And hungry sinner;
Give wine, give meat,
No matter whose;
Take from her feet
The very shoes,
And when her shoes had gone to others,
Fetch forth her sister's and her mother's.

She could not quit.
She had to share;
Gave bit by bit
The silverware,
The barnyard geese,
The parlor rug,
Her little niece—
'S christening mug,
Even her bed to those in want,
And then the mattress of her aunt.

An easy touch
For poor and lowly,
She gave so much
And grew so holy
That when she died
Of years and fame,
The countryside
Put on her name,

And still the Isles of Erin fidget
With generous girls named Bride or Bridget.

Well, one must love her.
Nonetheless,
In thinking of her
Givingness,
There's no denial
She must have been
A sort of trial
To her kin.
The moral, too, seems rather quaint.
*Who* had the patience of a saint,
From evidence presented here?
Saint Bridget? Or her near and dear?[68]

On one level, the Saint Bridget of Phyllis McGinley's poem commits "wrongs" against her own family members by taking their possessions without their permission. But on another level she did this in order to benefit those whose needs were greater. We might say, then, that Bridget's family members were called upon to bear patiently the wrongs Bridget did to them because she brought them face to face with their own lack of compassion for the poor.

Regardless of whether we think Bridget's actions were justifiable or not, her story illustrates that it is not just crotchety, mean, and insensitive people who do "wrongs" to others. Even those who live with saints, virtual saints, or just really good people can find themselves on the receiving end of "wrongs" that they are called to "bear patiently."

Perhaps the ultimate lesson here is that what we perceive as "wrongs" may or may not be actual "wrongs," and we may be the last ones capable of judging one way or the other. Perhaps the only position open to one who would "bear wrongs patiently" is to give up trying to decide whether actions we find hurtful or offensive are "wrongs" or not. Perhaps the best position we can take—when it comes to being on the receiving end of ordinary, everyday rudeness, insensitivity, and the like— is one of nonjudgmental patience and nonretaliation.

Apart from genuinely abusive relationships, then; and apart from social actions for social justice and the like that we discussed above, in terms of ordinary, everyday interpersonal "wrongs," we find ourselves called to act in ways consistent with the example of Christ. When he was accused falsely he set the example of what it means to "bear wrongs patiently."

In a few words, Thomas Merton suggested what is perhaps the best stance anyone can adopt who would take seriously this spiritual work of mercy. His words can be easily adapted to the topic of this chapter. He wrote:

> Nothing is more suspicious, in a man who seems holy, than an impatient desire to reform other men.
>
> ....
>
> Pay as little attention as you can to the faults of other people and none at all to their natural defects and eccentricities.[69]

## CHAPTER 13

# To Forgive All Injuries

This is another instance where it will be helpful if we make sure we understand our basic terms—in this case "forgive" and "injuries." First, the notion of forgiveness is one that tends to be rather vague. A regular dictionary offers this definition:

1. To excuse for a fault or an offense; pardon. 2. To renounce anger or resentment against. 3. To absolve from payment of (a debt, for example).[70]

A theological dictionary, on the other hand, expands the notion of forgiveness to that of "forgiveness of sins":

A central belief in the Jewish-Christian understanding of God's merciful dealings with us....Jesus forgave sins...and empowered his church to do the same....The forgiveness of sins through baptism...and in other ways requires repentance from us and the willingness to forgive those who sin against us....[71]

Clearly, the spiritual work of mercy that is the subject of this chapter is not limited to the first definition. Rather, for this work of mercy our forgiveness of one another is intimately related to God's forgiveness of us. There is no separation of divine forgiveness and human forgiveness. Thus, for this work of mercy the bottom line motivation for our forgiveness of others is the experience of God's forgiveness of us.

Forgiveness is no superficial notion. Rather, forgiveness is "the act of being restored to a good relationship with God, others, and self following a period or incident of sin or alienation."[72] For the Christian tradition, forgiveness means acceptance of the unconditional mercy of God through Christ and the ongoing readiness to pass along this experience to others by accepting them and by "forgiving all injuries." Therefore, the spiritual work of mercy we reflect on in his chapter is central to any Christian life.

The second key word is "injuries." It's interesting that this work of mercy does not say that we are to forgive others' sins against us. Rather, it uses the term "injuries." What's up, here? Let's turn again to our regular dictionary:

1. Damage or harm done to or suffered by a person or thing: escaped from the accident without injury; a scandal that did considerable injury to the campaign. 2. A particular form of hurt, damage, or loss: a leg injury. 3. Law. Violation of the rights of another party for which legal redress is available.[73]

This is as much help as we're going to get, as our theological dictionary includes no information about the term "injury." This fact by itself, however, may shed further light on why this spiritual work of mercy uses a distinctly nontheological term. For the realm in which we are to forgive is precisely that of the everyday and the ordinary. There is no sense in which we can understand this spiritual work of mercy as limited to some "spiritual" or ethereal realm. Rather, this work of mercy transcends or overcomes our habitual dichotomy between the physical and spiritual, or between the religious and the ordinary. Here, smack in the middle of our ordinary lives, is where this work of mercy is to be lived. It is precisely "injuries" that we are to forgive, meaning any way in which someone else truly hurts us, whether it be a physical, emotional, or ethical injury; whether it be an intentional or an accidental injury.

About now you may be laughing out loud. If you're at all in touch with "the real world," at least, you *should* be laughing out loud. After all, we live in what is sometimes called a "litigious society." Our's is a culture in which—on the social level, at least—the natural response to an injury is to sue the offending party or agency for as much money as you can get. Of course, often such situations aren't as simple as that. Sometimes it turns out that the only way to get a corporation or government agency to change is by means of a lawsuit.

One spring morning a woman decided to ride her bicycle to her sister's house, a few miles away. The weather was sunny and warm, and she thought that the ride would be good exercise. In the course of her ride she came to an intersection where she had to cross a railroad track that ran at an angle to the street she needed to cross. As she rode across the tracks her bicycle's front tire slipped into the space between the railroad track and the street, and the next thing she knew she was lying on the street with a badly throbbing ankle.

A passing motorist gave the woman a ride to a hospital where she learned that her ankle was broken. After a surgeon had used surgical screws and a metal plate to hold her ankle bones together, the woman lived with a cast on her leg for three months. Her summer certainly turned out to be different than she had planned.

Now, it would seem that if this woman was to put into practice the spiritual work of mercy called "to forgive all injuries" she would need to simply forgive the county and railroad agencies that had failed to keep the railroad crossing in good repair so it could be crossed safely by both pedestrians and cyclists. Unfortunately, that's not how things work in our society.

As it turned out, the county government and the railroad company are motivated to keep railway crossings safe primarily by the threat, and the actual bringing, of lawsuits. Unless the woman whose ankle was broken sued the county and railroad company the chances were that the crossing would have little concern for keeping such locations in good repair and safe for crossings. At first, the woman was reluctant to sue the county and the railroad company precisely because she wanted to act in a way consistent with the spiritual work of mercy that is the topic of this chapter. Once she realized, as he said, "how things work in the real world," however, she changed her mind. For the sake of cyclists and pedestrians in the community, the woman sued the county and the railroad company and—after a long, frequently frustrating legal process—she ended up with a relatively large amount of money for her trouble. As the woman's lawyer explained it, "You are entitled to compensation for your pain and inconvenience."

So much for trying to "forgive all injuries," right? Discussions with Catholic friends and some reading led the woman to conclude that, in fact, the entire process she had gone through had little, if anything, to do with the spiritual work of mercy that encourages us to "forgive all injuries." She decided that what happened to her was an accident that resulted from improper maintenance of a railway crossing, but no one let this happen specifically to cause her an injury. "It's all just 'business,'" she said.

> Like it or not, it's how the world works. It's a kind of
> goofy game played by corporations and governments, and
> if you don't play by their rules they'll take advantage

of ordinary people every time. It's not people relating to people. It's people trying to live with huge, impersonal agencies, and the only way you have any influence to change or improve things, when they need to be improved or changed in some way, is by means of the legal system, and that means litigation. It's crazy, but that's the way it is. Money is all these huge corporations and government agencies understand.

The scriptural and spiritual tradition behind the idea of forgiving injuries has to do with interpersonal relationships, and that's where it can best be understood and applied. As we noted at the beginning of this chapter, it also has meaning in the context of efforts to bring about social change by means of nonviolent action. But most of the time the "injuries" this spiritual work of mercy refers to are the simple, everyday hurts we cause one another as we go about our lives in the context of family, work, school, and daily social interactions.

Once again, an excellent way to understand this spiritual work of mercy is the tradition of the *imitatio Christi*, the imitation of Christ. Because we are members of his mystical body, his way of being present in the world, it is through our Christlike presence that Christ has an impact on our little corner of the world. Thus, without our ever saying a word about it, Christ is present when we make the effort to "forgive all injuries." And if we would be honest about it, we would need to admit that, more often than not, the "injuries" we receive come in the form of insensitive or cruel words from other people. Here is what *The Imitation of Christ* says about this. Jesus speaks to the disciple:

My son, stand firm and trust in Me. Words, after all, are only words. They dart through the air but they hurt no one; they can't even put a scratch on a stone.

If you are guilty of some wrong doing, think about willingly correcting yourself, and if you are unaware of any fault on your part, then think about gladly enduring these stinging words for the sake of God.

To put up with a few harsh words now and then is nothing great when you are still incapable of enduring harsh blows.

Why do you make such trifling matters into a mountain? Because you still have a worldly outlook and pay more attention to others' opinions than you should. You are afraid that men may ridicule you and hence you are willing to be taken to task for your faults, and so you make excuses to cover up your actions.

Take a good and thorough look at yourself and you will find that the world still resides in you and that you still foolishly desire to please men. Since you refuse to be taken down from your pedestal and be censured for your wrongdoings, it is obvious that you are not really humble, or dead to the world, nor *is the world crucified to you* [Gal 6:14].

Pay attention to My words and you will not care about the *ten thousand words* [1 Cor 14:19] that come from men. If all that human malice could possibly excogitate were uttered against you, what harm could all that do if you just let it pass you by and consider it nothing more than rubbish? All such talk can't do as much as pluck a single strand of hair from your head.[74]

Here the particular wisdom of the *Imitation* points out the extent to which we tend to overvalue the words of others, not only when the words are hurtful but, we might observe, when they constitute flattery, or even genuine praise. What matter the words of others, whether they hurt or not? In a very real sense, one of the best ways to "forgive all injuries" is to simply let them roll off your psyche like water off a duck's back. Of course, this is not to say that this is ever an easy thing to do. But it's a goal to aim for.

Of course, the ultimate model for learning to "forgive all injuries" is that of Christ himself. Recall the account from the Gospel of Luke:

> When they came to the place that is called The Skull, they crucified Jesus there with the criminals, one on his right and one on his left. Then Jesus said, "Father, forgive them; for they do not know what they are doing" (22:33–34).

In other words, even in situations where the person or persons who "injure" us seem to be fully conscious of and intentional about their cruelty or vindictiveness toward us, with Christ we can pray, "Father, forgive them; for the do not know what they are doing."

At the same time, we can look to the lives of various saints down through the centuries for examples of how this spiritual work of mercy has been lived out in various times and places. One of the most dramatic examples from modern times comes from Saint Edith Stein, a German philosopher, university professor, convert to Catholicism and a Carmelite nun. Edith died in Auschwitz, one of the notorious World War II Nazi death camps, but not before she showed a heroic capacity to "forgive all injuries." One who knew Edith Stein wrote:

> I will never forget the conversations I had with this genuinely Christian philosopher when time and time again she would insist that hatred must never be given the last word. Somehow it had to be possible—through prayer and atonement—to obtain the grace of conversion for those who hated. Hadn't Jesus, when he prayed

for those who hated him, those who crucified and
pierced him, turned his wounds into the symbol of love
that proved to be stronger in the end?[75]

Saints such as Edith Stein make it clear to us that this business of forgiving all injuries is not a matter of merely cultivat-
ing a pious attitude of some sort. Indeed, there are situations
where it can mean—as it did for Edith Stein—the willingness
to give up one's life with forgiveness in your heart for those
responsible for your death. We may smile with affection at the
true story of Saint Thomas More (1478–1535), the best-known
victim of the persecution of England's King Henry VIII against
Catholics who refused to accept royal supremacy over the
church in England. When he was condemned to death—based
on testimony from a lying witness, no less—More expressed
the hope that he and his judges would "hereafter in heaven all
meet merrily together, to our everlasting salvation."[76]

Again, this is an example of someone who could "forgive
all injuries" in the ultimate sense. But it was not the end for
Thomas More. As he approached the Tower of London, to be
imprisoned, More was met by the lieutenant of the Tower and
by the porter. According to custom, the porter asked that each
new prisoner give him his "upper garment." Thomas prof-
fered the porter his hat, saying "I am very sorry it is no better
for you."

"No, sir," the porter replied. "I must have your gown."
More's most recent biographer comments: "More would have
known perfectly well the tradition of hading the man his gown,
and his offering of the hat may be construed as an example of
that humour which always emerged in the most grave situations."[77]

Thomas More's forgiveness, it seems, often came in the
form not of a solemn expression of forgiveness but in the form
of joking around. The stairs to the scaffold were rather loose

boards so one of the officers present helped More to climb them. Later it was reported that More quipped, "When I come down again let me shift for myself as well as I can."[78]

As he approached the block where the headsman stood waiting to rid More of his head, "he asked the bystanders to pray for him in this world, and he would pray for them elsewhere."[79] Then showing how complete was his forgiveness of Henry the VIII for the great injustice he had done him, an eyewitness account reported that More "begged them earnestly to pray for the King, that it might please God to give him good counsel, protesting that he died the King's good servant but God's first."[80]

Finally, Thomas More's forgiveness extended even, and in an especially personal way, to his executioner. As was the custom, the headsman knelt before More to beg his pardon and blessing. "More kissed him, and is reported to have said, 'Thou wilt give me this day a greater benefit than ever any mortal man can be able to give me. Pluck up thy spirits, man, and be not afraid to do thine office.'"[81]

It is but a further proof of the good humor with which Thomas More extended forgiveness to all concerned that his last words were a caution to the executioner to not cut off his beard as it had done no one any harm.[82]

All such stories, as those of Saint Thomas More and Saint Edith Stein are, of course, accounts of heroic forgiveness of injuries. One is tempted to say that such heroic virtue is, however, not as difficult as simply living out this spiritual work of mercy in an everyday way in an everyday, ordinary life. This runs in the same vein as the observation—not without truth— that it is more difficult to live for one's faith than it is to die for one's faith.

Regardless, including in one's everyday spirituality the constant inclination or tendency to "forgive all injuries" is far from easy, as common as "injuries" are in the average, ordinary life.

Those we love do us injuries, some of which are intended, some not. People we do not know, whom we encounter daily in our ordinary comings and goings, they do us injuries, too, some intended, some not. But the point is that there can never be too much forgiveness of injuries, and the more we can put this spiritual work of mercy into practice, the more the love of God becomes real in our little corner of the world.

## CHAPTER 14

# To Pray for the Living and the Dead

Essentially, this spiritual work of mercy is the one that recommends intercessory prayer—that is, prayer for the good of others, both those among the living and those who have passed through the thin veil that separates this life from the next. All Christians believe in intercessory prayer for the living, but generally speaking Protestants do not believe that prayer does any good for those who have died. The Roman Catholic and eastern Orthodox Churches, going back to the days of the early Christians, have always taught that our prayers on behalf of those who have died can make a difference for them. This belief implies, of course, the reality of purgatory, about which the *Catechism of the Catholic Church* comments:

> All who die in God's grace and friendship, but still imperfectly purified, are indeed assured of their eternal salvation; but after death they undergo purification, so as to achieve the holiness necessary to enter the joy of heaven.
>
> The Church gives the name *Purgatory* to this final purification of the elect....[83]

The only reason we would want to pray for those who have died is to help and support them while they are "in" purgatory. There is no time or place in eternity, of course. But the mystery of life after natural death somehow includes the continued existence of relationships between those in this life and those in the next life. It also includes the possibility that we can help them by our prayers just as they can help us by their prayers.

Orthodox priest Father David Moser explains the understanding of his church in this way:

> ...most Protestant confessions teach that the judgment after death determines the eternal state of the soul. Not so, according to the Tradition and teaching of the Orthodox Faith. The particular judgment immediately after death only determines the state and "residence" of the soul in the spiritual world and that judgment is based on who our spiritual "friends" are. Do we have more converse with angels or demons? Do we devote ourselves more to the saints or to sinners? Are we attached to the world or to the Kingdom of God? Do we act like Satan or Christ? Whatever we are like, there we are placed in the spiritual world. And the demons are diligent in attempting to demonstrate that we are tied to them and not to Christ and so any and every unconfessed sin, no matter how seemingly small and insignificant is brought out by them as accusations against us and the angels on the other hand counter this accusation by a description of our righteous deeds which indicate our change of heart and life. But do not confuse this particular judgment and temporary disposition with the eternal disposition of the soul to be determined at the Great Judgment. Then, the soul being reunited with the body thanks to the general resurrection, each

person will be judged by God Who sees within either the spark of grace or none and those who have that spark will be brought into the Kingdom of God and those who do not will be cast into outer darkness—finally and eternally. So you see that when we pray for the departed, we do so knowing that the final judgment has not yet occurred and while we don't know what the exact needs of the departed are, we can simply lift them up to God calling out for His mercy.[84]

Father Moser's explanation relies on legitimate but mythic images from Scripture and sacred Tradition. Another approach is to explain intercessory prayer in contemporary theological terms. Take, for example, this explanation from a contemporary Catholic dictionary of spirituality:

Humanity's full incorporation through baptism into the Body of Christ...makes this mode of prayer a possibility and a responsibility for all the Church. This truth finds traditional expression in the dismissal from the Eucharistic assembly of all the unbaptized before the general intercessions, which complete the Liturgy of the Word. Petitions for the living and the dead in the Eucharistic Prayers attest to the constitutive role of this prayer form.

The practice of intercessory prayer is evident in the Hebrew Scriptures, where God is seen to raise up great intercessors such as Abraham, Moses, the prophets, kings, and priests who, rooted in God's covenanted fidelity, call the people back to God and intercede for them in their sin. This call often marginalizes the religious leader, and this the paradigm of intercessory prayer in the Hebrew Scriptures is the Suffering Servant (Isa 53:4—5:12).[85]

Add to this the example from the gospels of Jesus' prayer and ministry for others and you see that prayer on behalf of others ultimately reveals the presence of divine love in both this world and the next.

Intercessory prayer was a taken-for-granted part of both Jewish and Christian life right up until the Protestant Reformation in the mid-sixteenth century. At that time the Protestant Reformers attacked the practice of intercessory prayer because they misunderstood the theology behind it and because the practice was being abused in some instances. The Catholic and eastern Orthodox belief in intercessory prayer is rooted in the ancient Christian belief that in both this life and the next we belong to the communion of saints. Thus, we can pray for one another in this life, and those who have died can and do continue to pray for us from the next life. This is why Catholic and eastern Orthodox Christians pray to the saints, as well as—in private devotional prayer—to departed loved ones. We ask for their prayers for our welfare just as we might have asked for their prayers when they were in this world, and we pray for them, as well. As the *Catechism* says:

> The mutual solidarity of all humanity in, with, and through Christ is not destroyed by the grave, and if the salvation of each is affected by that of every other, then our prayerful concern for those who have gone before us in death is legitimate and necessary.[86]

It is important, of course, to always keep uppermost in mind that intercessory prayer, to remain valid, must never become an attempt to circumvent or disregard God's absolute sovereignty. Neither may we forget that the mediation of those who have died depends upon and mediates the grace of Christ who is our sole mediator with God our loving Father. Anything accomplished through intercessory prayer is accomplished by God's grace, not by any authority or power alone, independent of God's grace on the part of those who pray.

Sometimes we can get ourselves into spiritual trouble when it comes to intercessory prayer by, in effect, not taking the mystery of it all seriously enough. Sometimes our attempts to grasp what's going on in the dynamics of faith leads to simpleminded thinking. Simplicity is good; simplemindedness is not. For example, sometimes we find ourselves using concepts of space and time that simply do not apply beyond this life. We may think of God as distant when it makes more sense to think of him as near. In fact, both notions are true and both notions are false. Still, "near" is the one we probably need to remind ourselves of more often than "far."

Effective intercessory prayer requires us to take to heart the fact that God's love cannot be thought of on a space/time continuum. God's love simply *is*, always and everywhere, in time and in eternity. Thus, we can't think that today's prayers mean that God will act in a certain way tomorrow. The fact is that we don't know exactly how prayer works in terms of time and space; we only know that it is consistent with God's will for us to pray for one another. How this works out in the divine scheme of things is and always will be mysterious.

Neither is God a "distant and impervious creator of immutable natural laws."[87] Rather, to paraphrase the famous words of Saint Augustine, God's love is closer to us than we are to ourselves. God's love is beyond the grasp of the human intellect. Still, our loving Father's love is more like than unlike the most authentic human love.

Another misunderstanding of intercessory prayer that we need to be watchful about is the implication that such prayer has a cause-and-effect nature so that we can somehow change God's mind by our prayers. Intercessory prayer does not mean twisting God's arm until he relents and does what we want him to do. Rather, we always need to keep in mind the words of Saint Paul that when we pray the Spirit prays in and through us in ways the human intellect cannot grasp:

> ...the Spirit helps us in our weakness; for we do not know how to pray as we ought, but that very Spirit intercedes with sighs too deep for words. And God, who searches the heart, knows what is the mind of the Spirit, because the Spirit intercedes for the saints according to the will of God. We know that all things work together for good for those who love God, who are called according to his purpose (Rom 8:26–28).

Intercessory prayer is love in action expressing our love for those for whom we pray, and our love is but a pale shadow of God's love. We can only bring to intercessory prayer the practice of Christians for more than two millennia whose faith has expressed itself in this way. We cannot understand how intercessory prayer works, but we can never overlook the words of Jesus in the Gospel of Luke:

> And he said to them, "Suppose one of you has a friend, and you go to him at midnight and say to him, 'Friend, lend me three loaves of bread; for a friend of mine has arrived, and I have nothing to set before him.' And he answers from within, 'Do not bother me; the door has already been locked, and my children are with me in bed; I cannot get up and give you anything.' I tell you, even though he will not get up and give him anything because he is his friend, at least because of his persistence he will get up and give him whatever he needs.
>
> "So I say to you, ask, and it will be given you; search, and you will find; knock, and the door will be opened for you. For everyone who asks receives, and

everyone who searches finds, and for everyone who knocks, the door will be opened" (11:5–10).

Jesus, in the Gospel of Luke, instructs us to express our needs to our Father in heaven, and he says that our prayers will be answered. Only a simpleminded interpretation of these words of Jesus will say that this means we will get anything and everything we ask for. Rather, the story Jesus tells, and his teaching, can only mean that our prayers are heard and our prayers will receive a response consistent with God's loving will and consistent with human freedom which God never takes away from us. Thus, for example, if we pray for the return to the Church of someone we love, God's grace is available to this person but he or she will never be forced to do anything. Still, we can't forget Jesus' encouragement to be persistent about our prayer. We should never stop praying as somehow our prayers and God's grace work together so that we should never give up hope.

Intercessory prayer, "for the living and the dead," is one of the most commonly practiced spiritual works of mercy. This is because we find ourselves so often with no other recourse. We seem naturally inclined to prayer especially at those times when it seems there is nothing else we can do when others are in need. When we can do little or nothing else for someone we *can* pray for him or her, and as Christians we believe that prayer is far from a futile activity. Indeed, intercessory prayer is a basic characteristic of a heart in tune with God's mercy. Intercessory prayer participates in the intercession of Christ himself. "In intercession, he who prays looks 'not only to his own interests, but also to the interests of others,' even to the point of praying for those who do him harm [1 Tim 2:1; see also Rom 12:14 & 10:1]."[88]

In other words, intercessory prayer is a basic act of unselfish love for others. At the same time, such prayer is never easy, especially if we keep in mind Jesus' teaching that we should be persistent about prayer. It can be difficult to keep praying, and keep praying, and keep praying, no matter how much time goes by. It can take heroic faith, hope, and love to be truly persistent in prayer.

The tradition of "making a novena" is one way that Catholicism helps people to be persistent about prayer. "Novena" comes from the Latin word for "nine"—hence, a novena consists of nine days of prayer for a specific purpose. There is nothing magical about the number nine, of course, the point is simply to encourage persistence in prayer. It takes a certain commitment and determination to pray even a formulaic devotional prayer nine days in succession. It takes persistence.

To shift our focus a bit, however, to pray for the living is one thing, while to pray for the dead is another thing. Sometimes to pray for the dead can seem fairly simple compared to praying for the living. The difficult part of praying for people who are still alive is that chances are good that you can observe whether your praying seems to have an effect or not. Say you pray for the return of a loved one to the Church. You can pray for years, even decades, and see no difference in the person's life. The living can be a genuine challenge when it comes to being persistent about prayer. Anecdotal accounts of wonders wrought by prayer may never seem to be borne out by your own experience. You pray for years and years, and the loved one never returns to the Church. Finally, maybe he or she dies and is still a "lapsed" Catholic. What good, you may ask yourself, were all the prayers you prayed for all those years?

In some cases, of course, we see our prayers answered in this life. There are many remarkable true stories about ways in which prayer seemed to make a noticeable difference in the lives of others. Miracles do occur. Loved ones away from the Church for many years return. But there are also many who will tell you that their prayers seemed to have no effect; nothing changed. In such instances, our prayers shift from being "for the living" to being "for the dead." Faith tells us that once a person has died there is no question about him or her being in God's loving care, but belief in purgatory tells us that now we can help our loved one through the transition, through the purification through which he or she must pass in order to be united fully and finally with our loving Father in heaven.

In the end, the mystery of "prayer for the living and the dead" is the same as the mystery of love in this life and the next. For what is prayer but love, in the most unsentimental sense, expressed for those we care about? When we pray for others we manifest our love for them, no matter whether they still inhabit time and space or have slipped to the veil between this life and the next. Our love for them is our love, of course, but it is also God's love for them. Or rather, our love for others becomes a "channel," as it were, for God's love for them. Thus, when we pray we express both our love and God's love, and the two blend into one love that is both human and divine.

Our relationships with others are real in this life, and they continue to be real eternally. Thus, when we pray for others among both the living and the dead we unite ourselves to them and bring God's love into the reality of their experience, or the "reality of their reality" whether they are in time or space or in eternity. This is, ultimately, what prayer is about. It's about God's love for those for whom we pray. To pray "for the living and the dead" is to unite ourselves to them in the mystery of God's love.

Nineteenth-century American psychologist William James (1842–1910), who called himself a "piecemeal supernatural-ist" rather than a religious person, understood the mystery of prayer better than many conventional believers. In his classic, *The Varieties of Religious Experience*, James described peti-tionary prayer as "not indeed a purely subjective thing;—it means a real increase in intensity of absorption of spiritual power or grace;—but we do not know enough of what takes place in the spiritual world to know how the prayer operates...."[89]

In his novel *In Heaven As on Earth: A Vision of the Afterlife*, M. Scott Peck, M.D., has his central character remark wisely:

> Prayer is funny stuff....On the one hand, I can't guarantee it will work. On the other, don't be disappointed if it seems not to. Sometimes good things can happen way later after the fact. God's schedule isn't necessarily ours, you know.[90]

Our final reflection, then, must be that "prayer for the living and the dead" is to be our concern and our practice. We pray for others because we are led by the Gospel and by sacred Tradition to do so, without ever expecting to understand precisely how it "works." We pray for others because, in the end, it is an essential way to manifest our love for God and neighbor. Beyond that, for the finite human intellect, there is only the holy mystery of prayer as an expression of a love that is both human and divine.

# Notes

## Introduction

1. "CCD" was short for Confraternity of Christian Doctrine, a program established to provide parish catechetical programs for children who did not attend Catholic schools. Nowadays, "religious education" is the preferred term. In some cases, however, a "rogue" parish uses the old Protestant term "Sunday School."
2. English translation of the *Catechism of the Catholic Church* for the United States of America, Second Edition (Washington, D.C.: United States Catholic Conference, Inc. Libreria Editrice Vaticana, 1994, 1997), nos. 362 & 365.
3. *Catechism of the Catholic Church*, no. 2447.

## Chapter 1

4. *Catechism of the Catholic Church*, no. 2269.
5. Ibid., no. 2831.
6. Susan Mulvihill, "Plant a Row grows crops for the hungry." The Spokesman-Review (Spokane, Washington, April 12, 2002: D3).
7. Rev. Francis J. Connell, C.SS.R., S.T.D., ed., *The New Confraternity Edition Revised Baltimore Catechism* No. 3 (New York: Benziger Brothers, Inc., 1949), 113.
8. Paul Thigpen, *A Dictionary of Quotes From the Saints* (Ann Arbor, Mich.: Servant Publications, 2001), 166.

## Chapter 2

9. See the Web site of the Clean Water Network, www.cwm.org.
10. On the Internet, go to http://www.paulsen.com/. (Original broadcast May 28, 1967.)
11. For an excellent in-depth discussion of faith as ultimate concern see Paul Tillich, *Dynamics of Faith* (New York: HarperCollins, 1957).

## Chapter 4

12. *The New Confraternity Edition, Revised, Baltimore Catechism.* "The text of the Official Revised Edition 1949 with Summarizations of Doctrine and Study Helps by Rev. Francis J. Connell, C.SS.R., S.T.D." (New York: Benziger Brothers, Inc., 1949), 113.
13. Dan Parkin, *International Socialist Review* (January-February 2002), 69.
14. John Scott Shepherd, *Henry's List of Wrongs* (New York: Rugged Land, 2002).
15. Shepherd, ibid., 70.
16. Michael Kennedy, *The Jesus Meditations: A Guide for Contemplation* (New York: Crossroad Publishing Co., 2002), 15.
17. Thomas Merton, *Selected Poems of Thomas Merton*, Enlarged Edition (New York: New Directions Publishing Corp., 1967), 130.

## Chapter 5

18. See the Human Rights Watch Web site at the following internet address: http://www.hrw.org/campaigns/refugees/index.htm.
19. See http://www.indcatholicnews.com/merl.html.
20. On the Internet, go to http://www.volunteerpathway.org/honorees/fuller.html.

## Chapter 6

21. On the Internet, go to http://web.wt.net/~cbenton/healing/h16.htm.
22. See Richard D. Smith, *Can't You Hear Me Callin': The Life of Bill Monroe* (Boston: Little, Brown & Co., 2000), 282–287.
23. Smith, ibid., 284.
24. Smith, ibid., 284.
25. Smith, ibid., 284.
26. Smith, ibid., 284.
27. Smith, ibid., 284.
28. Smith, ibid., 284.
29. Smith, ibid., 284.
30. Smith, ibid., 285.
31. *Catechism of the Catholic Church*, Glossary.
32. On the Internet, go to http://www.mywhatever.com/cifwriter/content/52/abcd2713.html.

## Chapter 7

33. On the Internet, go to http://www.hospicefoundation.org/what_is/.
34. See ibid.
35. Kathy Saunders, "At the Hour of Our Death." *U.S. Catholic*, February 1998.
36. See *Catechism of the Catholic Church*, no. 2301.
37. Thomas Lynch, *The Undertaking: Life Studies from the Dismal Trade*. (New York: Penguin Putnam, Inc., 1997), 112–113.
38. Ibid., 113.
39. Ibid., 118.

## Chapter 8

40. *The American Heritage Dictionary of the English Language*, Third Edition (New York: Houghton Mifflin Co., 1996).
41. Gerald O'Collins, S.J., and Edward G. Farrugia, S.J., *A Concise Dictionary of Theology*, Revised and Expanded Edition (Mahwah, N.J.: Paulist Press, 2000), 243–244.
42. *The American Heritage Dictionary of the English Language*, Third Edition (New York: Houghton Mifflin Co., 1996).
43. On the Internet, go to http://www.intervention.com/servsfi.html.

## Chapter 9

44. Robert F. Delaney, "Ignorance." *The Catholic Encyclopedia*, Volume VII. Copyright © 1910 by Robert Appleton Company. Online Edition Copyright © 1999 by Kevin Knight. See http://www.newadvent.org/cathen/07648a.htm.
45. André Dubus, *Broken Vessels* (Boston: David R. Godine, 1991), 194.
46. Ron Hansen, "Faith and Fiction," in *A Stay Against Confusion* (New York: HarperCollins, 2001), 26.
47. A prime example of the latter is the *Left Behind* series of novels by Tim LaHaye and Jerry B. Jenkins (Tyndale House Publishers). These novels are allegorical fiction based on a fundamentalist interpretation of the New Testament book, Revelation. LaHaye's and Jenkins' novels make the unprovable assumption that Revelation is a document filled with predictions about the future, an assumption that Catholic and mainline Protestant methods of Bible interpretation reject on historical and scientific grounds.
48. Graham Greene, *The Heart of the Matter*, in Philip Stratford, ed., *The Portable Graham Greene*, Revised Edition (New York: Penguin Books, 1994), 304–305.

49. André Dubus, "A Father's Story" in *In the Bedroom: Seven Stories by André Dubus* (New York: Vintage Books, 2002), 136.
50. Ibid., 136.
51. Flannery O'Connor, *Mystery and Manners* (New York: Farrar, Straus and Giroux, 1961), 172–173.

## Chapter 10

52. Richard P. McBrien, general editor, *The HarperCollins Encyclopedia of Catholicism* (San Francisco: HarperSanFrancisco, 1995), 433.
53. Ibid.
54. Ibid.
55. Gerald O'Collins, S.J., and Edward G. Farrugia, S.J., *A Concise Dictionary of Theology*, Revised Edition (Mahwah, N.J.: Paulist Press, 2000), 67.
56. See Mitch Finley, *What Faith Is Not* (Franklin, Wis.: Sheed & Ward, 2002).
57. Richard Abanes, *One Nation Under God: A History of the Mormon Church* (New York: Four Walls Eight Windows, 2002), 412.
58. *Catechism of the Catholic Church*, no. 1790.
59. O'Collins, S.J., and Farrugia, S.J., ibid., 117.

## Chapter 11

60. "From the Oscar Romero Catholic Worker House in Oklahoma City, on the 27th Sunday in Ordinary Time in the year of our Lord 2001." See http://www.justpeace.org/warprayer.htm.
61. For a wonderful film adaptation of *Silas Marner* see "A Simple Twist of Fate" (1994) starring Steve Martin.
62. George Eliot, *Silas Marner: The Weaver of Raveloe* [1861] (New York: Penguin Classics, 1967), 70.
63. Traditional. This arrangement and lyrics are as sung by the Soggy Bottom Boys in the film *Oh Brother, Where Art Thou?* See http://www.aadcom.com/askjeeves/rotation/dating.htm.

## Chapter 12

64. Thomas à Kempis, *The Imitation of Christ*, 3:XIX. Trans. by Betty I. Knott (London: Collins Fontana, 1963).
65. For an overview of the many aspects of spousal abuse as an issue consult this Internet Web site: http://www.extension.ualberta.ca/legalfaqs/nat/v-spo-en.htm.
66. Ibid.
67. Ibid.

68. Phyllis McGinley, *The Love Letters of Phyllis McGinley* (New York: Viking Press, 1954), 50–53.
69. Thomas Merton, *New Seeds of Contemplation* (New York: New Directions, 1961), 255.

## Chapter 13

70. Excerpted from *American Heritage Talking Dictionary*. Copyright © 1997 (The Learning Company, Inc.). All rights reserved.
71. Gerald O'Collins, S.J., and Edward G. Farrugia, S.J., *A Concise Dictionary of Theology*, Revised Edition (Mahwah, N.J.: Paulist Press, 2000), 92.
72. "Forgiveness," in Richard P. McBrien, general editor, *The HarperCollins Encyclopedia of Catholicism* (San Francisco: HarperSanFrancisco, 1995), 534–535.
73. Excerpted from *American Heritage Talking Dictionary*. Copyright © 1997 (The Learning Company, Inc.). All rights reserved.
74. Thomas à Kempis, *The Imitation of Christ*. Edited and translated by Joseph N. Tylenda, S.J. (New York: Random House, 1998), III:46.
75. Johannes Hirschmann, S.J., "Schwester Teresia Benedicta vom Heiligen Kreuz," in *Monatsschrift des Bundes Neudeutschland*, 34. Jg. 1981, pp. 125–126. Quoted in Waltraud Herbstrith, *Edith Stein: A Biography*. Trans. by Father Bernard Bonowitz. OCSO (San Francisco: Harper & Row, 1985), 113.
76. Quoted in Richard P. McBrien, *Lives of the Saints* (San Francisco: HarperSanFrancisco, 2001), 253.
77. Peter Ackroyd, *The Life of Thomas More* (New York: Doubleday, 1998), 365.
78. Ibid., 405
79. Ibid.
80. Ibid.
81. Ibid.
82. Ibid.

## Chapter 14

83. *Catechism of the Catholic Church*, n. 1030–1031. In his novel, *In Heaven As on Earth: A Vision of the Afterlife* (New York: Hyperion, 1996), M. Scott Peck, M.D., acknowledges "the Roman Catholic Church for keeping the vision of Purgatory alive...."
84. Father David Moser of Saint Seraphim of Sarov Orthodox church, Boise, Idaho. The quotation is from an Orthodox Web site: http://www.orthodox.net/articles/about-prayer-for-the-dead.html.

85. Andrew D. Ciferni, O.Praem., "Intercession" in Michael Downey, ed., *The New Dictionary of Catholic Spirituality* (Collegeville, Minn.: The Liturgical Press, 1993), 543.

86. Ibid., 543.

87. Ibid.

88. *Catechism of the Catholic Church*, n. 2636.

89. William James, *The Varieties of Religious Experience* [1902]. New York: Dover Publications, 2002), 467.

90. M. Scott Peck, ibid., 206.